The Diet Game: Playing For Life!

by

Marci Page Sloane MS, RD, LD/N, CDE

First published by AuthorHouse 06/29/04

ISBN: 1-4184-6814-2 (e-book)
ISBN: 1-4184-2218-5 (Paperback)

Library of Congress Control Number: 2004091648

Printed in the United States of America
Bloomington, IN

This book is printed on acid free paper.

www.TheDietGame.net; www.MarciSloane.com

MARSH Affinity Group Services-a service of Seabury & Smith-American Dietetic Association recognized malpractice insurance

Comic Strips, Illustrations, Cover Design and Layout by Randy Gossman

Photograph by Tammy Taylor; 3-D cover by Jorge Verea; Editing by Jeanette Cézanne

Information in this book is for informational purposes only. It is not intended as a substitute for advice from your own medical team. The information is not to be used for diagnosing or treating any health concerns you may have – please contact your physician or health care professional for all your medical needs. Check with your physician before making any changes in your diet or exercise.

Every accomplishment starts with the decision to try
-Anonymous

This book is dedicated to my loving mother and friend,
Doris Garfinkel,
who will always be with me

Table of Contents

Acknowledgements

I would like to thank my patients for inspiring me to write *The Diet Game*. Helping people reach their goals of weight loss and improved health has brought a great deal of value into my life. They, in turn, have motivated me to win at my own diet game. All the people who have tolerated my neuroses while writing this book should get an award!

I would like to start by thanking Jeannette Cézanne and Randy Gossman for enhancing the presentation of this book. Jeannette not only edited *The Diet Game* but also acted as psychological counselor while I was living through the rewrites! And Randy's creative illustrations, comic strips and cover design added a light touch to serious health issues. He not only added his delightful humor but also introduced me to Tammy Taylor, a fine photographer, who shot the front cover photo, Lloyd Morley who assisted in proper lighting and Jorge Verea, an incredible 3-D artist.

I need to acknowledge my father, Paul, who was the nutrition editor throughout the first draft; Lois, my stepmother, who started promoting this book before it was even written; and my friend Kim, who joined me in the diet game and completely transformed herself by making the decision to eat reasonably and exercise vigorously, so the woman who had been hiding for so many years could finally come alive again. I also want to thank Terry for being such a great source of inspiration and proving to me that people can accomplish anything they set their minds to. And, of course, my deepest gratitude to Jon, my husband, who always encourages me to be the best I can be.

Foreword

I am a very lucky person: I met Marci Sloane, my savior! Dramatic as that may sound, Marci literally has saved my life – or, more appropriately, has helped motivate me to want to save my own life. I am a big girl and always have been since the age of eight.

Marci is a dietitian on a mission. She's not only a good listener but she clearly explained what I needed to do to avoid the consequences of my actions. She opened my eyes to what I had been putting in my body!

I realize that it was my commitment that moved me closer to my goal weight. However, it was Marci's persistence, dedication and compassion that helped drive me to it. I can't say I would have had such positive results with any other dietitian. Knowing that Marci had to struggle along with the rest of us was a great help to me. I knew she understood how arduous the battle to be healthy was. Through her supportive nutritional guidance, her sense of humor and her no-nonsense approach to permanent weight loss, I have been able to educate myself, change my behavior and take off over eighty pounds!

Thin blondes can be intimidating; Marci is not... she is a very down-to-earth, genuine and warm person who really cares about people. She makes it FUN to lose weight. Thank you so very much, Marci! I really could not make this important journey without your help!

- **Terry Fleishman**

Preface

Hello, and congratulations! Thank you for making a healthy choice by purchasing this book. You must be one of the countless people who have yo-yo dieted for many years, and are probably feeling frustrated right now. But help is in sight! *The Diet Game* is here to teach you how to stop dieting, once and for all. It's time to put down the endless collection of hard-to-follow and even harder-to-live-by diet books. It's time to learn, via a straightforward and easy approach, healthy ways to eat and cook, while at the same time avoiding the many debilitating diseases that plague our country. I've included simple-to-prepare recipes for those who don't especially like to cook (like me!), as well as healthy eating tips, 30 days of practice menus for the non-dieter who is ready to make permanent lifestyle changes, and nutritional guidance for those wanting to live long, healthy and happy lives. Let's play this game for life!

Why should you listen to me? Because I did it myself! I am a Registered Dietitian, licensed in the state of Florida since 1996, as well as a Certified Diabetes Educator since 2000. I studied at Teachers College at Columbia University in New York City and received a double Masters of Science degree in Nutrition and Physiology in 1996. Aside from these credentials, I have been a nutritional counselor for the past seven years and I have seen the consequences people suffer when they abuse their bodies with food. Consequently, I have spent ample time learning about how to eat right to avoid these devastating outcomes; I know how to lose weight permanently by making choices one can live with for a lifetime. I've examined the fad diet theories, the quick weight-loss schemes, science, and my experience in counseling thousands of people who have confided in me what lead them to their successes and failures so I can bring to you what really works!

My Story: There were a number of major changes in my life that led to my own weight gain during the four and a half years I spent working toward a master's degree. I got married, changed careers, relocated, and spent eighteen months watching my mother fight to survive ovarian cancer. In June of 1996, during the time of finals and graduation, my mother slowly succumbed to the disease.

My life had become overwhelming to me. I lost my focus and gained more than thirty pounds; and I did so even after earning a degree in nutrition! I was very uncomfortable with the extra weight, but I refused to buy clothes in a larger size – instead, I wore stretch pants with big, long tops to hide my weight. I felt awful in my overweight, unhealthy body and I knew I needed to change!

The first step I took was to join a gym. I tried at the beginning to use the treadmill every day for an hour, but that really didn't work for me – I felt like a rat running in a wheel! I realized that I couldn't make this leap into good health without some sort of support system, so I joined the gym's exercise classes. I quickly became friends with many people who had goals similar to mine. Every day we grumbled and moaned and had a great time as we moved closer to achieving our objectives. If I missed a class, everyone would ask me where I had been, and I felt more committed because of that. During that time, I did lose some inches, but I lost very little weight. How frustrating! What was I doing wrong?

My second step, I realized, had to be the food part of the equation: I was still eating too much. I was trying to make healthy choices when I ate, but I still liked to eat a lot of food. I also wasn't paying close attention to hidden calories. I had to accept the fact that I will always crave certain foods, and I will always like to eat a lot of food, and neither of those things is ever going to change.

What I had to do, instead, was reprogram the way I *behaved* toward food. It was time to start thinking about what lower-calorie foods I could eat that would allow me to continue eating a lot and feel satiated. I needed to stop buying those foods that I could not control myself around.

I did it a day at a time, trying each day to be mindful of what I was putting in my mouth. I kept reminding myself of the benefits. Think of it as a game, I told myself: the game of life. And it was also a game of balance. What did I want most? To eat recklessly and feel good during those short moments, or to become a conscientious consumer and be healthy and feel good for the rest of my life? It was that simple. It was my choice, and I was ready to succeed!

In only two and a half months – just ten weeks! – after exercising, changing my behavior and eating more sensibly, I lost the thirty extra pounds I had gained. That's an average of three pounds a week. I couldn't believe it! I was now feeling and looking good. I felt empowered by all the attention my new "look" was getting – everyone was noticing!

Now, at the age of forty-one, I am at my strongest, healthiest and most confident. Sometimes I think back on how much time I wasted being unhappy as I spent worthless hours blissfully gorging myself. Had I only weighed out the pros and cons of overeating, I might have done some things differently.

These days, I continue to exercise daily. I no longer attend the gym, but I have turned instead into an exercise tape/DVD junkie, which is a lot of fun. My food choices and my passion for exercise have helped me maintain my weight for several years now, and I don't see that ever changing. Being rewarded by my daily accomplishments feels much better than the moments of bliss poor food choices bring. My choices, along with my exercise habits, are automatic now. Exercising is part of my routine. I brush my teeth, shower and exercise... *every day*. Making healthy food choices is not a difficult task. After all, the rewards are endless. *You can do it, too!* And I'm here to help you get there!

According to the 2000 National Health and Examination Survey (NHANES), two-thirds of American adults are overweight or obese (see body mass index, provided further on in the book). With all the diets available, there is still an obesity epidemic! The common trend I see in the majority of people who have been unsuccessful at losing weight is that they *go on diets*. People believe in diets; they "know" it's a way to lose weight. So the first thing we need to recognize is that *diets do not work*! We all know this, yet we find ourselves believing their promises anyway.

There are no miracles: sorry. The secret to losing weight and maintaining weight loss is to focus on lifestyle and behavioral changes. People are making a lot of money on our desperate need to lose weight. Our frustration with yo-yo dieting has led us to believe the ridiculous promises and so-called miracles that are presented to us daily. The diet pills, diet books, exercise machines and special foods are appealing – but do they work? Think about it: if they really worked, would the majority of people in this country still be overweight?

The problem is that diets are *only temporary solutions to permanent problems*. The true issue lies deep inside you, and it's up to you to find it within yourself to succeed. I believe you have the ability to achieve your goal; but first you must commit to making choices that will allow you the success you are striving for. The good news is that you have the power to do so! It is already inside you. Face it – no fad diet, weight loss surgery or diet pill can do it for you. You need to understand why you precipitate your unhappiness through weight gain and ill health – otherwise, you may never be ready to change your destiny and reach your goals.

I am here to empower you. I am here to help you look inside and make the choices you need to make in order to be free to live your life healthfully and happily. I know the strength is there! There are no easy answers, but if we work together, we can override temptation with determination.

If you want something, you need to work hard for it. The Ds you need are determination and desire – *not* diet and certainly not deprivation. Those Ds set us all up to fail! Losing and maintaining weight requires continual thought, commitment and even a little creativity! Instead of offering you the typical "miracle" diet that simply does not exist, I am offering you ways to eat – whether you are at home, on the run or dining out – that will keep you satiated and even healthy!

The Diet Game provides a month of practice meal plans to assist you in your new way of eating – to help you along on your journey. This is not meant to be a short-term diet but rather a teaching tool (a game!) for you to finally learn how to eat well for the rest of your life. Some meal plans may work better for you than others. Repeat those days as often as you wish. Pay attention to what you are eating and how it makes you feel. The meal plans must be reasonable for you. Use them to guide yourself. If you desire an occasional cookie or piece of cake it's important for you to allow yourself that. It's more important for you to think about eating those foods moderately when you do – but to not deprive yourself of them completely. I want you to succeed so please don't forget that you're a human being! *The Diet Game* includes many delicious, filling, low-calorie, healthy, fast and easy-to-prepare recipes, as well as a discussion of natural ways of controlling conditions such as high cholesterol and hypertension that you may not know about.

You need to find a way to be comfortable with your new eating habits. Believe me, because I have had to do the same thing; in fact, I continue to struggle to make the right choices. I am not one of those lucky people who are naturally thin; I have to work hard every single day to make the right food choices. It isn't easy. But it *is* worth it! You will feel better about yourself because you will have accomplished a goal, you will be looking great, and you will be a lot healthier.

I believe that anyone can change, and that includes you! I will help to motivate you and show you easier ways to make food choices – while enjoying your meals at the same time. The miracle occurs when you take your life into your own hands and fight for it! Don't surrender to temptation. You're smarter and stronger than that: I know you are! What you need to do is find a place where food can be enjoyed without deadly consequences. I have found that place and I want to share it with you.

Together, we can do this! Get ready to change your life!

Come on! It's time to be the person you want to be! Follow me, and let's play *The Diet Game, for life!*

> Your journey to improved health and happiness begins right now!
>> Be good to yourself!
>> Marci Sloane

Chapter One: Understanding The Diet Game

Introduction

Sloane's Secrets for Success:
Think before you eat!

So what's the secret? Here it is: you can lose weight by sustaining your appetite with non-refined carbohydrates (high fiber, whole grains) and by combining these carbohydrates with lean protein (fish, poultry, lean meats) and/or monounsaturated fats (olive oil, nuts, avocado).

Instead of relying more heavily on protein, as most popular diets are recommending, I want you to increase monounsaturated fats. Too much protein increases the workload for your kidneys. Not only that, but the protein most people choose contains saturated fat and cholesterol; this may increase your risk of heart disease as well. Saturated fat encourages the liver to make harmful cholesterol and also clogs your arteries. Your cholesterol will be lower simply from weight loss, although your arteries will still be getting clogged. Excessive protein may also leach calcium out of your bones, and that can lead to osteoporosis. But by increasing monounsaturated fats, you will be able to sustain your appetite and lose weight more efficiently in the same way protein would allow you to without the possible dangers and as current research is finding – you will reap healthy benefits as well!

The American Heart Association, American Diabetes Association, Adult Treatment Panel III of the National Cholesterol Education Program and other nationally-recognized health organizations suggest that lower carbohydrate intake combined with higher fat intake (primarily from monounsaturated fats) helps to reduce the risk of heart disease and can reduce triglycerides and increase HDL (healthy) cholesterol levels in people with metabolic syndrome. The Centers for Disease Control and Prevention has determined that at least 47 million Americans – about one in five people – have metabolic syndrome, also known as syndrome X, pre-diabetes or insulin resistance. Metabolic syndrome is diagnosed when a person has three or more of the following conditions: abdominal obesity (or the "apple shape" – men with over 40" and women with over 35" waist circumference), high triglycerides (150 mg/dL or higher), low HDL cholesterol (men with 40 mg/dL or lower and women with 50 mg/dL or lower), high blood pressure (130/85 or higher), and high fasting glucose levels (110 mg/dL or higher). These people are at high risk for developing type 2 diabetes and heart disease. In the July 23, 2003 issue from the Journal of the American Medical Association (JAMA), monounsaturated fats, soy and soluble fiber were suggested to work as effectively as statins (cholesterol-lowering drugs) to lower cholesterol and heart disease risk. Update: The International Expert Committee has published revised guidelines in November 2003 that lower the diagnosis of pre-diabetes or metabolic syndrome from 110 mg/dL to 100 mg/dL. This will add 20% to the 47 million Americans who already have metabolic syndrome. Obesity greatly increases the incidence of metabolic syndrome.

The prevalence of metabolic syndrome and obesity in this country may explain why heart disease is the number one killer in America. Because of the pervasiveness of this condition, *The Diet Game* provides 40% of your daily calories from mostly non-refined carbohydrates, 25% of your daily calories from very lean or lean protein, and 35% of your daily calories from primarily monounsaturated fats.

What does this all mean?

Let's take the theories behind some fad diets and apply them to healthy eating. Dr. Atkins had a point when he claimed that by eating protein and fat and little to no carbohydrates you could lose weight. Why does this work? Protein and fat sustain your appetite because they get digested very slowly. Carbohydrates get digested quickly and also hold onto water in the body. Quick weight loss comes from water loss and eating fewer calories – due to the fact that you are satiated sooner and you are not eating the refined carbohydrates (found in white flour) that encourage your appetite!

Carbohydrates (starch, fruit, milk, vegetables) provide most of your nutrients! They are your main source of energy, strengthen the body to ward off disease, and provide fiber and calcium and vitamins and minerals. If you use and don't abuse them, you can maintain a healthy weight and consume all the food groups in moderation. Choosing primarily fruits and vegetables (mostly water and fiber, low-calorie foods you eat more moderately than starches) as your carbohydrate selections will allow you to lose weight more efficiently! It is unrealistic and unhealthy to eat mostly protein and fat for the rest of your life!

Just think... you can stay healthy AND conquer your weight problem by simply using certain foods, or food combinations, to satisfy your appetite!

Of course, you then need to convince yourself not to eat just for the sake of eating – the "head hunger" versus "stomach hunger" problem. This leads to regret and to being overweight and unhealthy.

Carbohydrates have a bad reputation because of the type most people consume. Carbohydrates that are refined, such as white bread, white pasta and white rice, digest very quickly. What actually happens when you eat these refined carbohydrates is that they break down into sugar or glucose in your bloodstream within one to two hours. Once they break down into sugar, your blood sugar rises and falls quickly. When the blood sugar falls, it encourages your appetite.

Why? Because sugar is energy. If your blood sugar (energy level) drops, then your brain tells your body to eat more so your energy level will rise. This is what is so BAD about carbohydrates! However, if you consume high-fiber carbohydrates like whole grains (such as kasha, bulgur, barley, millet, whole-wheat pasta, oats, and brown rice), then you can consume less and still feel satisfied, since your blood sugar level will be sustained over a longer period of time. This is the same principle used by the high-protein, high-fat, low-carbohydrate diets. It's all about how to sustain your appetite most efficiently and safely!

What I have done in this book is give you lots of ideas about how to use these "slow-to-digest foods" to your advantage. By consuming primarily high-fiber carbohydrates and combining lean protein and/or unsaturated fat with carbohydrates, you will sustain your appetite and eat less. Most importantly, you will be adding more nutrients to your diet and you will not be omitting any food groups (as so many fad diets suggest you should). Furthermore, it's a more reasonable way to eat for the rest of your life! This is not a temporary diet; instead, it is a behavioral and lifestyle change! Using low-calorie, non-starchy vegetables as fillers to your meals is another secret to successful weight loss and good health. Instead of having two cups of whole wheat pasta you can have one cup with one cup of broccoli and onions. This decreases the calories while providing extra bulk to satisfy your appetite.

Try also to consume fluids to fill up your stomach. Low-sodium V8 or tomato juice, broth-based lower sodium soups, water, and herbal iced teas are some terrific alternatives. Better still, they all count toward your eight-plus glasses of water for the day!

The Diet Game: Instructions

For One or More Adult Players –
AIM: Achieving permanent weight loss!
OBJECTIVE: Collecting the most points in 30 days as you reach your goal weight in record time and maintain it for life!
REWARD: Spending money saved from extra food, clothes in different sizes, medications, or doctor bills on a vacation, spa treatment, buying new clothes for the last time, joining a gym, taking tennis lessons, and, of course, buying *The Diet Game* for all of your friends and loved ones!

If you have a competitive spirit, play with a friend and see who wins!

GETTING STARTED:
Step on the wheel (scale). Decide what number you want to see and how many miles (calories) you need to travel on your journey through *The Diet Game*. Read the introduction to move in the right direction on your road to understanding the basic concept of how to eat for good health and satiety.

Once you calculate how many miles (calories) you need to lose weight you can join Stella, Marci, Dottie or Randy on their journey to good health! Follow the spaces (pages) in order to familiarize yourself with the food serving sizes and to guide yourself through some food decisions.

Jump to food labels so you learn how to substitute various foods at your meals.

Always use your budget of carbohydrates, protein and fat to better understand how much or how little you need to be eating every day. This is easier than counting calories. Therefore, the recipes provide only serving sizes. The concept of combining slow-digesting foods like high fiber carbohydrates with lean protein and/or monounsaturated fats is critical. 30 days of sample or suggested menus are provided to guide you through your journey.

You may pick the appropriate meal plan, start at Day One and follow for 30 days to win! The first two weeks omit starch at your dinner meal and nighttime snack to help speed up the weight loss process. Weigh yourself on Day One first thing in the morning, in the nude. Weigh yourself on Day Seven the same way. If you have not lost weight, then go back to Day One! Try to always weigh yourself once a week, at the end of each week, and at the same time of day.

Use the food, exercise and feeling journal to increase your awareness of your actions and to make you accountable for them as well. Duplicate as needed.

Use the weekly tracker by checking off the appropriate boxes (C= one carbohydrate serving, P= one protein serving, and F= one fat serving) as you consume your servings. Learn healthy eating in 30 days and you will be able to *play for life!* Duplicate the daily or weekly tracker as needed.

Feel free to repeat days with more desirable food choices if you would like. I want this to be as pleasant for you as possible, so you can win *The Diet Game!*

Reward system: Gain points by the choices you make. For each healthy food choice, you gain one point per serving. For each unhealthy food choice, you deduct one point per serving. Bonus points: If you complete a day with only healthy food choices, you gain an additional point per day (see total points for specific calorie meal plans in chapter 3). Record numbers of points in your food, exercise, and feelings journal.

HEALTHY SERVING + 1	UNHEALTHY SERVING -1
Protein: very lean, lean	Protein: Medium fat (except for eggs and tofu), high fat
Carbohydrate: non-refined, high fiber, low glycemic index or load	Carbohydrate: refined, processed, high glycemic index or load
Fat: unsaturated, primarily mono and omega 3 fats	Fat: saturated or trans fat

The Diet Game: Playing by the Rules

Rule #1: Think before you eat! You have choices with consequences. Decide what outcome you really want. *Check with your doctor before beginning this program.*

Rule #2: Remember to limit or avoid refined carbohydrates like starches without fiber: white bread, white rice, pasta, low-fiber cereals (*Special K, Rice Krispies* or *Cornflakes*, to name a few), and replace them with high-fiber foods like whole-grain bread, brown or wild rice, whole-grain pasta, *Shredded Wheat n' Bran* or oatmeal, sweet potatoes, kasha, and barley. Refined foods encourage your appetite, whereas dense/high-fiber/low glycemic index (see glycemic index) foods discourage it by filling you up.

Rule #3: Combine foods such as high-fiber carbohydrates, lean protein and monounsaturated fats to sustain your appetite efficiently. They also offer many healthy benefits. Making a trail mix of high-fiber cereal and nuts or seeds will sustain your blood sugar and discourage you from eating excessively. You'll be surprised at how little you need to eat before you feel satiated!

Rule #4: Use fluids to fill yourself up. Always consider having low-sodium V8 or tomato juice, club soda or water, herbal iced tea, green tea, 25-calorie fat-free hot cocoa or vegetable soup to fill you up before you start munching on chips or sweets. You may include the 25-calorie fat-free hot cocoa or coffee as a free choice once or twice daily. If you desire an alcoholic beverage be sure to count it in the appropriate calories and be moderate.

Rule #5: Eliminate or cut back on refined foods so you will no longer crave them and your weight loss will be less challenging. These carbohydrates encourage your blood sugar to fluctuate and this increases the desire for more of them. Put that bag of pretzels down!

Rule #6: All fish dishes may be substituted with tofu (bean curd), poultry, pork tenderloin or lean meat. Prepare your grilled or baked protein with spices and flavors such as garlic, basil, lemon juice, mustard, or light teriyaki sauce. Fish and tofu are the best choices since they both provide many health benefits. However, if you have had breast cancer, or are at high risk for it, please indulge in tofu and other soy products only three times per week.

Rule #7: For faster weight loss, omit starches with your dinner meal and limit them throughout the day. Use non-starchy vegetables (frozen or fresh) and fruits as your main carbohydrate sources, since they provide water and fiber and will flush and cleanse your body. Always bulk up sandwiches with lettuce, tomato, and other vegetables (this is considered a free choice). Don't like vegetables? Try different ways to prepare the ones you can tolerate and you may be surprised that you can really enjoy them! Perhaps you can sauté them in garlic and olive oil, steam them in chicken broth or vegetable bouillon, add salsa or stewed tomatoes or even add low fat cheese!

Rule #8: Follow your appropriate carbohydrate, protein and fat budget. You may always substitute one serving for another of your choice, as long as they have the same value. You may choose rye bread, whole wheat or even sourdough bread or pick one high fiber cereal (5 grams or higher) for another. If you don't like nuts you may substitute them with another healthy fat. Be sure to use the concept of "slow-digesting foods" to aid in weight loss by sustaining your appetite.

Rule #9: Start exercising and progress to at least 45 minutes for five days a week. Combine cardiovascular exercise such as walking or bicycling with toning and resistance training such as weight lifting, squats, sit-ups, lunges, and push-ups. Resistance training allows you to replace fat with muscle so your metabolism will speed up and you will lose weight most efficiently.

Rule #10: Your new mantra is: Increase high-fiber carbohydrates, non-starchy vegetables, monounsaturated and omega 3 fats, and mostly protein from fish and soy. Decrease refined and processed carbohydrates, sweets and saturated and trans fats.

The Diet Game

by Randy Gossman

Determining Caloric Requirements

Body Mass Index

Body Mass Index (BMI) has gained popularity over the past few years. It is a mathematical equation that gives a number to the relationship of your height and weight. The American Dietetic Association uses the following BMI formula: multiply your weight in pounds by 700. Then divide that number by your height in inches two times.

For example: a person weighs 135 pounds and stands 5'7" tall. 135 pounds x 700 = 94,500. Divide that twice by 67" (5'7"). 94,500/67 = 1,410 divided by 67 again = BMI is 21

BMI was designed to determine how your weight affects the status of your health. Too high a BMI means that you are more prone to illnesses such as heart disease, cancer and diabetes. A pear-shaped person, who has excess weight in their hips and thighs, is at a much-decreased risk of many diseases than is an apple-shaped person, who has much of his or her weight in the chest and abdominal area.

What number do you hope to see?

BMI	WEIGHT	RISK (pear)	RISK (apple)
<18.5	Underweight	N/A	N/A
18.5–24.9	Normal	N/A	N/A
25 – 29.9	Overweight	Increased	High
30 – 34.9	Obese	High	Very High
35 – 39.9	Obese	Very High	Very High
>40	Very obese	Extreme	Extreme

Determining your Body Mass Index (BMI)

Below is a table to easily figure out your BMI:

BM	19	20	23	24	25	29	30	35	40
HEIGHT	WEIGHT (IN POUNDS)								
58"	91	96	110	115	119	138	143	167	191
59"	94	99	114	119	124	143	148	173	198
60"	97	102	118	123	128	148	153	179	204
61"	100	106	122	127	132	153	158	185	211
62"	104	109	126	131	136	158	164	191	218
63"	107	113	130	135	141	163	169	197	225
64"	110	116	134	140	145	169	174	204	232
65"	114	120	138	144	150	174	180	210	240
66"	118	124	142	148	155	179	186	216	247
67"	121	127	146	153	159	185	191	223	255
68"	125	131	151	158	164	190	197	230	262
69"	128	135	155	162	169	196	203	236	270
70"	132	139	160	167	174	202	207	243	278
71"	136	143	165	172	179	208	215	250	286
72"	140	147	169	177	184	213	221	258	294
73"	144	151	174	182	189	219	227	265	302
74"	148	155	179	186	194	225	233	272	311
75"	152	160	184	192	200	232	240	279	319
76"	156	164	189	197	205	238	246	287	328

Calorie Requirements and Weight Determination

To find out what size your frame is:

Place your thumb and index finger around your wrist. If your finger overlaps your thumb, you have a small frame. If your finger touches your thumb, you have a medium frame. If your finger does not touch your thumb, you have a large frame.

To find out how much you should weigh:

Men:
√ 106 pounds for the first 5 feet and 6 pounds for each addition inch thereafter. For example: A man who stands 6' or 72":
♦   106 for the first 5 feet and 12 inches x 6 pounds (for each additional inch)
= 106 + 72 = 178 pounds

♦   For a small frame: subtract 10%
♦   For a medium frame: keep the number
♦   For a large frame: add 10%

Women:
√ 100 pounds for the first 5 feet and 5 pounds for each addition inch thereafter. For example: A woman who stands 5'7" or 67":
♦   100 for the first 5 feet and 7 inches x 5 pounds (for each additional inch)
= 100 + 35 = 135 pounds

How many calories should I eat to maintain my weight?

Many, many formulas exist for determining adequate calories to maintain your weight! ***The simplest one is the following***:

Gender	Activity Level	Multiply your weight in pounds by this number
Male	Inactive	13
Male	Active	15
Female	Inactive	10
Female	Active	12

Example: I weigh 135 pounds and exercise five times each week. 135 x 12 = 1620, so I need approximately 1620 calories to maintain my weight. Since one pound equals 3,500 calories, to lose one pound a week, I must subtract 500 calories a day from that total (1120). In addition, my exercise consists of about 30 minutes of kickboxing a day plus weights. I burn about 400-500 calories a day. Now I can lose 2 pounds a week. Weight loss varies significantly from one person to another.

The *Harris Benedict Equation* (you'd have to be Einstein!) is the most precise estimate using a mathematical formula to determine your calorie requirements, and it is very specific. It uses your height, weight, age, activity level and gender to find the calories you need to maintain your current weight. As you will see there are slightly different formulas for men and women.

W= weight in kilograms. 1 kg = 2.2 pounds (take your weight in pounds and divide by 2.2)
H= Height in centimeters. 2.54 cm = 1 inch (take your height in inches and multiply by 2.54)
A= Age in years

Men: 66.5 + (13.75 x W) + (5.003 x H) – (6.775 x A) =

Women: 655.1 + (9.563 x W) + (1.850 x H) – (4.676 x A) =

Use the following example for a woman:
A 41-year-old woman who weighs 135 pounds, stands 5'7" tall and exercises moderately:
W= 135/2.2 = 61 kg
H= 5'7" or 67" = 67 x 2.54 = 170 cm
A= 41 years

655.1 + (9.563 x **61**) + (1.850 x **170**) –(4.676 x **41**) =
655.1 + 583 + 315 – 192 =
1553 – 192 = 1361 calories required per day to maintain weight (does not include activity level)
1361 x **1.5** = 2042
(total calories required per day to maintain weight)

Multiply this for your activity level:

Activity Level	Exercise per week
1.2	Sedentary or inactive
1.4	Light exercise 1-3 times
1.5	Moderate exercise 5 times
1.7	Strenuous exercise 6-7
1.9	Very strenuous exercise 6-7

The above equations are estimations of your metabolic rate. A new FDA-approved, handheld portable device is now on the market that provides the most accurate measure of your metabolic rate (the number of calories needed to maintain weight during rest). The *MedGem*, sold by Mead Johnson, performs a 10-minute breathing test and is available in many health clubs and dietitian's offices.

Calorie expenditure during one hour of exercise:
AL = Activity Level   # = weight in pounds
L = Low M = Moderate H = High   V = Vigorous

Exercise	AL	130 #	160 #	190 #
Aerobics	L	295	350	430
Aerobics	H	410	500	600
Bicycling	L	355	425	525
Bicycling	M	475	565	700
Bicycling	V	600	700	865
Stationary Bike	L	325	385	475
Stationary Bike	M	400	500	600
Stationary Bike	V	620	740	900
Calisthenics	L-M	265	315	385
Calisthenics	V	475	565	700
Cleaning	L-M	150	175	215
Cleaning	V	265	315	385
Dancing	M	265	315	385
Kickboxing	M	600	700	860
Jump rope	L	470	565	700
Jump rope	M	600	700	860
Running	L	475	565	700
Running	M	650	775	950
Running	V	825	985	1200
Swimming	L	235	280	345
Swimming	M	475	565	700
Swimming	V	600	700	865
Tennis	M	475	565	700
Walking	L	150	175	215
Walking	M	200	250	300
Walking	V	235	280	345
Water sports	M	175	215	260
Weight lifting	L-M	175	215	260

Food Serving Size List

Each food listed is one serving. Pay close attention to calories *and* portion sizes. This is a learning experience. After your month of practice meals, you will no longer need to depend on this book to know how to eat!

PROTEIN (P): each serving has 7 grams or 1 ounce:

Very lean protein has 0-1 gram of fat and 35 calories
Beans (1/2 cup also counts as 1 carbohydrate serving)
Cheese: Fat-free or low-fat or ¼ cup of soft cheese
Egg whites (2) or egg substitutes (1/4 cup)
Fish: Scrod, flounder, fresh tuna or canned in water
Poultry: Chicken and turkey (white meat, no skin)
Shellfish: Clams, crab, lobster, scallops, shrimp

Lean protein has 2-3 grams of fat and 55 calories
Beef: Flank steak, London broil, tenderloin, roast beef
Cheese: 3 grams of fat or less, grated Parmesan (2 Tbsp.)
Fish: Salmon, swordfish, 2 medium sardines
Lamb: Roast or lean chop
Liver: (high in cholesterol)
Lunch meats or hot dogs with 3 grams of fat or less
Pork: Lean pork tenderloin, ham, Canadian bacon
Poultry: Chicken or turkey (dark meat, no skin)
Veal: Roast or lean chop

Medium-fat protein has 5 grams of fat and 75 calories
Beef: Any prime cut, corned or ground
Cheese with 5 grams or less fat per ounce
Egg (1 whole)
Fish: Any fried fish product

Pork: Top loin, chop
Poultry: Chicken or turkey (dark meat with skin, or fried
Tofu (1/2 cup)

High-fat protein has 8 grams of fat and 100 calories
Cheese: American, Cheddar, Monterey Jack, Swiss
Other: Lunch meats such as bologna and salami
Hot dog
Bacon (3 slices)
Peanut butter (1 Tbsp.)
Pork: Spareribs, ground pork, pork sausage

CARBOHYDRATES (C): each serving has 15 grams

Starch: *servings have approximately 80 calories*
Bread
Mini 1-ounce bagel - ½
Large bagel - ¼
Bread (reduced-calorie) - 2 slices
Bread (white, whole-wheat, rye, etc.) - 1 slice
English muffin, pita, hot dog/hamburger bun - ½
Small roll - 1
Tortilla (small) - 1
Waffle - 1

Cereals and grains
Bulgur, kasha, millet (cooked) - ½ cup
Cereals (unsweetened, ready to eat) - ¾ cup
Cornmeal or wheat germ (dry) - 3 Tbsp.
Couscous, pasta, rice (cooked) - 1/3 cup
Flour (dry) or breadcrumbs - ¼ cup
Granola, low-fat - ¼ cup

Grits, Oatmeal, *Wheatena*   (cooked) - ½ cup

Starchy vegetables
Baked beans - 1/3 cup
Beans, corn, peas, plantains - ½ cup
Potato (sweet or white) - 3 ounces or small
Potato (mashed) - ½ cup
Squash (winter: acorn, butternut, etc.) - 1 cup

Crackers and Snacks
Animal Crackers, Graham crackers, saltines - 6
Matzo - ¾ of a piece
Melba toast - 4 slices
Oyster crackers - 24
Popcorn - 3-4 cups popped
Snack chips (pretzels, tortilla, potato) - 15 chips

Fruit: *servings have approximately 60 calories*
Servings equal approximately 1 cup fresh fruit, small to medium-sized whole fruit, ½ cup canned (without the juice), 4 oz. fruit juice, ¼ cup dried and 1 Tbsp. jam or jelly

Milk: *12 grams of carbohydrates, 8 grams of protein*
8 ounces of milk (skim, 1%, 2% or whole), ½ cup evaporated milk, 1/3 cup dry milk, ¾ cup plain non-fat yogurt, non-fat or low-fat fruit-flavored yogurt

Milk	Fat (grams)	Calories
Skim Milk	0 - .5	90
1 %	2.5	110
2%	5	120
Whole	8	150

Non-starchy (low-carbohydrate vegetables):
Each serving has 5 grams for ½ cup cooked or 1 cup raw and 25 calories

Artichoke, asparagus, bean sprouts, beets, broccoli, Brussels sprouts, cabbage, carrots, cauliflower, celery, collards, (kale, mustard, turnip greens), cucumber, eggplant, leeks, green beans, mushrooms, okra, onions, peapods, peppers, radishes, lettuce, sauerkraut, scallions, spinach, tomatoes, zucchini

FATS (F): each serving has 5 grams and 45 calories

Monounsaturated fats
Avocado, medium - 2 Tbsp. (1 ounce)
Oil (canola, olive) - 1 tsp.
Olives (black/green) - 8-10 large
Almonds, Cashews - 6 nuts
Peanuts - 10 nuts
Pecans - 2 nuts
Peanut butter - ½ Tbsp.
Sesame seeds - 1 Tbsp.

Polyunsaturated fats
Margarine or mayonnaise - 1 tsp.
Low-fat margarine, low-fat mayonnaise - 1 Tbsp.
Walnuts - 2 nuts
Oil (corn, soy, safflower) - 1 tsp.
Salad dressing - 1 Tbsp.
Salad dressing, light - 2 Tbsp.
Seeds (pumpkin, sunflower) - 1 Tbsp.

Saturated fats
Butter (stick) - 1 tsp.
Butter (whipped/light) - 1 Tbsp.
Coconut - 2 Tbsp.
Cream, Half-and-Half - 2 Tbsp.
Cream cheese - 1 Tbsp.
Cream cheese, light - 2 Tbsp.
Shortening/Lard - 1 tsp.
Sour Cream - 2 Tbsp.
Sour Cream, light - 3 Tbsp.

Source: American Dietetic Association Exchange List

Eating Out

When you dine out, please continue to use your common sense. Make reasonable choices for continued success. Here are some suggestions:

Chinese Food: Shrimp, chicken, pork or beef with vegetables. Do not get breaded or fried choices. Ask for your food dry, with little sauce, or get it steamed. The sauce has hundreds of calories, lots of salt, sugar, fat and cornstarch. Get white rice (or brown when available) and don't eat more than 2/3 cup (cooked). Each 1/3 of a cup of cooked rice is about 80 calories (and that is for steamed rice, not fried!). Eat the inside of the egg roll and watch all the extra sauces like duck sauce and soy sauce that you add. Have the soup, but only have a few fried noodles if you must. Refrain from the ice cream most of the time and have pineapple and a fortune cookie.

Italian food: If you have veal, chicken, or shrimp Parmesan, do not get cheese on top. This saves a quick 500 calories (500 calories x 7 days a week is the pound you will lose at the end of the week!). Have your side dish of pasta and one roll, or forego the pasta and have a double order of vegetables. Have a salad with the vinaigrette on the side, or a clear vegetable or bean soup. If the meal is very large, bring some home. Learn to consume smaller portions, and then your calorie consumption will be lower.

Mexican food: Forgo the nachos most of the time. Try to limit cheese dishes and fried dishes. (Ask if you are not sure which ones are fried.) After all, full-fat cheese is 100 calories per slice. Choose the shrimp, vegetable, or chicken fajitas. Ask them to leave off the sour cream and provide only one or two tortillas instead of 4 (then there is no temptation). You may have the guacamole. Instead of refried beans, ask for black beans. If you must have nachos, do not overeat them. The cheese, meat, avocado and sour cream have many, many calories. The avocado (guacamole) is the healthiest of the choices therefore enjoy it without all the rest!

Japanese food: Have sushi, steamed dumplings, and teriyaki dishes. Do not overuse the soy sauce or any sauces – remember that sauces carry the majority of fat, salt and/ or sugar. Have a miso soup or a salad and an entrée. Japanese food is usually one of the lower-calorie choices you can make. You will be sure to have fewer calories if you eat Japanese food more often than other types. However, you might ask for the teriyaki sauce on the side. Be careful of over-consuming sushi. The rice adds up in calories and it is a refined carbohydrate.

Continental Cuisine: Always have a salad to fill up on. If you have a piece of bread or a roll, do not eat your potato. Order your protein with a double order of vegetables, and make sure they are not swimming in butter. Do not have dessert just for the sake of having it. After a full meal, you should not be hungry – therefore, there is no need for dessert! Get out of that habit! Have coffee or a skim-milk cappuccino instead.

Reading Food Labels

Nutrition Facts ● 1

Serving Size 1 cup (253g) ● 2
Servings Per Container 4

Amount Per Serving

Calories 260   Calories from Fat 70 ● 3

● 4   **% Daily Value***

Total Fat 8g ● 5	**13%**
Saturated Fat 3g	**17%**
Cholesterol 130mg ● 6	**44%**
Sodium 1010mg	**42%**
Total Carbohydrate 22g ● 7	**7%**
Dietary Fiber 9g	**36%**
Sugars 4g	

Protein 25g ● 8

Vitamin A 35%	●	Vitamin C 2%
Calcium 6%	●●9	Iron 30%

*Percent Daily Values are based on
a 2,000 calorie diet. Your daily
values may be higher or lower   ● 10
depending on your calorie needs:

Calories: 2000 2,500

Total Fat	Less than	65g	80g
Sat Fat	Less than	20g	25g
Cholesterol	Less than	300mg	300mg
Sodium	Less than	2,400mg	2,400mg
Total Carbohydrate		300g	375g
Dietary Fiber		25g	30g

Calories per gram: ●11
Fat 9 ● Carbohydrate 4 ● Protein 4

1. Nutrition facts: This tells the consumer that the FDA has approved this label.
2. The serving size represents all the quantities of nutrients listed on the label. If you're consuming 2 cups of this particular food, there will be 16 grams of fat. The grams in parenthesis indicate how much the serving size weighs.
3. Calories from fat are usually rounded off. By multiplying the total fat (in this case, 8 grams) by the number of calories in each gram of fat (9 calories) the result will be the total calories from fat. 9 x 8 = 72 calories from fat. This number was rounded down to 70.
4. % Daily Value is explained near the (*) asterisk. It is based on a 2,000-calorie diet. This may not be suitable for everyone. On a 2,000-calorie diet, your total fat intake should be less than 65 grams. Therefore, the total fat of 8 grams listed is 13% of the total daily value of fat or 13% of 65 grams is eight grams.
5. The total fat figure includes all fats: saturated, polyunsaturated and monounsaturated. These three fats should add up to the total. If they don't, the remainder can be from trans fat (only if there is partially hydrogenated oil in the ingredient list) or from a smaller amount of fat (.5 or ½ a gram) that is not required to be listed.
6. Cholesterol should not exceed 300 mg per day. If you have heart disease, limit your cholesterol intake to 200 mg per day. The yolk of one egg has 215 mg of cholesterol. Eggs do, however, contain ample vitamins and minerals. Consume fewer than four a week if you have heart disease or diabetes.

7.   Total carbohydrate turns completely into sugar except for the dietary fiber part. In this case, nine grams of fiber may be subtracted from the total carbohydrate to find the amount of sugar this product will actually breakdown into. Only 13 grams of total carbohydrate will turn into sugar in your bloodstream within one to two hours. The four grams of sugar listed come from refined sugar found in this product. The number of grams of carbohydrates you would count is 13 grams, which would include the refined sugar while subtracting the non-digestible fiber.

8.   Protein is listed in grams. However, we think of protein in terms of ounces. Seven grams is equal to one ounce of protein on the food label. In this case, there are 25 grams of protein. This is equal to approximately 3 ½ ounces of protein.

9.   This product offers six percent of your total calcium allowance for the day.

10.   See #4

11.   There are more than twice the calories in each gram of fat than in each gram of carbohydrate or protein.

♦ All bolded words contain the categories underneath them. Total fat contains all types of fat indented and in lighter print underneath it whereas Total Carbohydrate contains dietary fiber and sugar.

♦ A low-fat food has three grams of fat or less per serving.

♦ A low-saturated-fat food has one gram or less per serving.

♦ A low-sodium food has 140 mg per serving or 400 – 600 mg per meal. Limit sodium consumption to 3,000 mg per day and at least 500 mg per day. If you are on a low-sodium diet due to hypertension or kidney disease consume fewer than 2,400 mg.

The Diet Game

by Randy Gossman

1,200 – 1,800 Calorie Meal Plans
Use these "handy" guides for easy measuring:

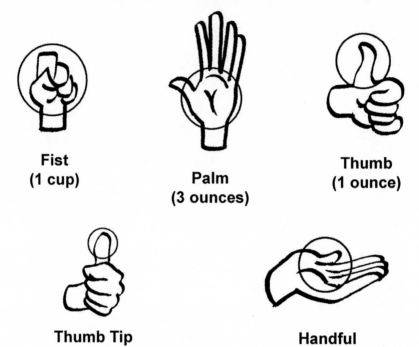

Fist
(1 cup)

Palm
(3 ounces)

Thumb
(1 ounce)

Thumb Tip
(1 tsp.)

Handful
(1-2 ounces)

For longer journeys add more energy:

Journeys	**Stella**	**Marci**	**Dottie**	**Randy**
Miles	1200	1400	1600	1800
Carbs 40%	8	9	11	12
Protein 25%	7	9	10	11
Fat 35%	5	6	6	7
Optimum Reward points	600	720	810	900
Optimum Bonus points	+ 30	+30	+30	+30

Weight loss varies depending on your metabolic rate, extent of exercise, how closely you follow meal plans, and other factors.

Stella's 1200-Mile Journey

Sample Daily Tracker

1200 Miles	Carbohydrate: 8 servings	Protein: 7 servings	Fat: 5 servings

You are allowed the following amounts of carbohydrates, proteins and fats. Choose them wisely! Check off the boxes as you consume each serving.

C=Carbohydrates (starch, fruit, milk, vegetables): 1 serving has 15 grams of total carbohydrate. Pick 8 servings. Refer to food serving size list.

15 g	15 g	15 g	15 g
15 g	15 g	15 g	15 g

P=Proteins (fish, poultry, meat, eggs, cheese, tofu, etc.): Choose mostly very lean or lean. 1 serving has 7 grams of protein or 1 ounce. Pick 7 servings.

7 g	7 g	7 g	7 g
7 g	7 g	7 g	XXXXXXX

F=Fats (oils, nuts, butters, etc.): Choose mostly monounsaturated fats. 1 serving has 5 grams of fat. Pick 5 servings.

5 g	5 g	5 g	5 g	5 g

W=Water

16 ounces	16 ounces	16 ounces	16 ounces

Stella's 1200-Mile Weekly Tracker

DAY 1	C	C	C	C	C	C	C	C
	P	P	P	P	P	P	P	
	F	F	F	F	F			
DAY 2	C	C	C	C	C	C	C	C
	P	P	P	P	P	P	P	
	F	F	F	F	F			
DAY 3	C	C	C	C	C	C	C	C
	P	P	P	P	P	P	P	
	F	F	F	F	F			
DAY 4	C	C	C	C	C	C	C	C
	P	P	P	P	P	P	P	
	F	F	F	F	F			
DAY 5	C	C	C	C	C	C	C	C
	P	P	P	P	P	P	P	
	F	F	F	F	F			
DAY 6	C	C	C	C	C	C	C	C
	P	P	P	P	P	P	P	
	F	F	F	F	F			
DAY 7	C	C	C	C	C	C	C	C
	P	P	P	P	P	P	P	
	F	F	F	F	F			

Always
think before you eat. This is one option.
The other is to eat without a conscience.
That only encourages obesity!

Stella's 1200-Mile Weekly Tracker

DAY 1	C	C	C	C	C	C	C	C
	P	P	P	P	P	P	P	
	F	F	F	F	F			
DAY 2	C	C	C	C	C	C	C	C
	P	P	P	P	P	P	P	
	F	F	F	F	F			
DAY 3	C	C	C	C	C	C	C	C
	P	P	P	P	P	P	P	
	F	F	F	F	F			
DAY 4	C	C	C	C	C	C	C	C
	P	P	P	P	P	P	P	
	F	F	F	F	F			
DAY 5	C	C	C	C	C	C	C	C
	P	P	P	P	P	P	P	
	F	F	F	F	F			
DAY 6	C	C	C	C	C	C	C	C
	P	P	P	P	P	P	P	
	F	F	F	F	F			
DAY 7	C	C	C	C	C	C	C	C
	P	P	P	P	P	P	P	
	F	F	F	F	F			

Did you remember to drink at least 8 eight-ounce glasses of water or herbal tea today?

Stella's 1200-Mile Weekly Tracker

DAY 1	C	C	C	C	C	C	C	C
	P	P	P	P	P	P	P	
	F	F	F	F	F			
DAY 2	C	C	C	C	C	C	C	C
	P	P	P	P	P	P	P	
	F	F	F	F	F			
DAY 3	C	C	C	C	C	C	C	C
	P	P	P	P	P	P	P	
	F	F	F	F	F			
DAY 4	C	C	C	C	C	C	C	C
	P	P	P	P	P	P	P	
	F	F	F	F	F			
DAY 5	C	C	C	C	C	C	C	C
	P	P	P	P	P	P	P	
	F	F	F	F	F			
DAY 6	C	C	C	C	C	C	C	C
	P	P	P	P	P	P	P	
	F	F	F	F	F			
DAY 7	C	C	C	C	C	C	C	C
	P	P	P	P	P	P	P	
	F	F	F	F	F			

Have you started your exercise program?

Stella's 1200-Mile Weekly Tracker

DAY 1	C	C	C	C	C	C	C	C
	P	P	P	P	P	P	P	
	F	F	F	F	F			
DAY 2	C	C	C	C	C	C	C	C
	P	P	P	P	P	P	P	
	F	F	F	F	F			
DAY 3	C	C	C	C	C	C	C	C
	P	P	P	P	P	P	P	
	F	F	F	F	F			
DAY 4	C	C	C	C	C	C	C	C
	P	P	P	P	P	P	P	
	F	F	F	F	F			
DAY 5	C	C	C	C	C	C	C	C
	P	P	P	P	P	P	P	
	F	F	F	F	F			
DAY 6	C	C	C	C	C	C	C	C
	P	P	P	P	P	P	P	
	F	F	F	F	F			
DAY 7	C	C	C	C	C	C	C	C
	P	P	P	P	P	P	P	
	F	F	F	F	F			

Believe
in yourself and you will succeed. Make reasonable
eating choices to last for a lifetime.

Stella's 1200-Mile 2-Week Shortcut

Day One	Day Two
Breakfast	**Breakfast**
1 whole-wheat English muffin (2 C)	1 cup cooked oatmeal made with water (2 C)
1 ounce of goat cheese (1 P)	1 Fruit (1 C)
Lunch	2 walnuts, chopped (1 F)
Large salad (1 C)	**Lunch**
2 ounces tuna (2 P)	2 slices whole-wheat bread(2C)
2 Tbsp. light dressing (1 F)	2 ounces turkey (2 P)
10 peanuts (1 F)	Lettuce and tomato
½ cup chickpeas (1 C) (1 P)	**Snack**
Snack	Baked apple (1 C)
1 fruit (1 C)	2 walnuts, chopped (1 F)
6 almonds (1 F)	**Dinner**
Dinner	Salad with 2 tsp. olive oil plus vinegar (2 F)
12 ounces low sodium V8 juice (1 C)	1 cup broccoli steamed with ½ cup no-salt canned diced tomatoes (1 C)
3 ounces shrimp grilled with spices (3 P)	5 ounces salmon, grilled with garlic and 1 Tbsp. of light teriyaki sauce (5 P)
1 cup cooked spinach with ½ cup no-salt diced tomatoes (1 C)	**Snack**
Snack	1 fruit (1 C)
12 almonds (2 F)	6 almonds, slivered (1 F)
1 fruit (1 C)	
25-calorie fat-free hot cocoa (free)	

Today is your first day. Make sure to weigh yourself so you will see your results!

Day Three	**Day Four**
Breakfast 1 cup cooked *Wheatena* made with water (2 C) 2 walnuts, chopped (1 F) Cinnamon	**Breakfast** 1 slice whole-grain bread (1 C) ¼ cup fat-free or 1% cottage cheese (1 P) 1 cup fresh fruit (1 C)
Lunch Caesar Salad *recipe* (1 C) (1 P) (2 F) Add 3 ounces shrimp (3 P)	**Lunch** 2 slices rye bread (2 C) 2 slices low-fat cheese (2 P) 2 slices tomato
Snack 12 ounces low-sodium V8 or tomato juice (1 C)	**Snack** 3-4 cups of popcorn (1 C)
Dinner 3 cups vegetables steamed in chicken bouillon (2 C) 3 ounces of scallops (3 P)	**Dinner** Salad with 2 Tbsp. light dressing (1F) 10 low-sodium black olives (1 F) 4 ounces fish or poultry (4 P) grilled with spices 1 ½ cup broccoli (1 C) 1 tsp. olive oil drizzled on top of steamed vegetables (1 F)
Snack 2 fruits (2 C) 12 cashews (2 F)	**Snack** 2 fruits (2 C) 12 almonds (2 F)

Are you using your weekly tracker for guidance?

Day Five	*Day Six*
Breakfast	**Breakfast**
1 English muffin (2 C)	2 frozen *Go Lean* low-fat, whole-grain waffles (2 C)
1 egg fried in *Pam* spray (1P) (1 F)	2 Tbsp. maple syrup (2 C)
1 slice low-fat cheese (1 P)	**Lunch**
Lunch	Large salad (1 C)
2 slices whole-wheat bread (2C)	3 ounces chicken (3 P)
2 ounces shrimp or chicken salad (2 P)	10 peanuts (1 F)
1 Tbsp. light mayonnaise (for salad) (1 F)	2 tsp. olive oil plus vinegar (2 F)
Snack	**Snack**
12 ounces low-sodium V8 juice (1 C)	1 cup carrots and celery (free)
Dinner	**Dinner**
1 Tbsp. olive oil (3 F) to sauté	3 cups vegetables steamed with 2 Tbsp. salsa (2 C)
3 cups vegetables (2 C) and	3 ounces shrimp, grilled or baked with spices (3 P)
3 ounces fish, poultry, or lean meat (3 P)	1 slice low-fat shredded cheese melted on top vegetables (1 P)
Snack	**Snack**
Sugar-free Jell-O (free)	¾ cup Kashi's *Good Friends* cereal (1 C)
1 fruit (1 C)	12 cashews (2 F)

Common sense.
Use it! You have been on countless diets
over the years that brought you temporary
success. Stop wasting time year after year.
Use that time to make permanent changes.

<u>**Day Seven**</u>	<u>**Day Eight**</u>
Breakfast	**Breakfast**
1 cup cooked oatmeal made with water (2 C)	2 slices bread (2 C)
1 small banana (1 C)	1 slice low-fat cheese (1 P)
	2 eggs, poached (2 P) (2 F)
Lunch	**Lunch**
Avocado, Shrimp, Roasted Garlic and Walnut Salad *recipe* (1 C) (3 P) (3 F)	Large salad (1 C)
	Vinaigrette Dressing *recipe* (2F)
Snack	½ cup grilled tofu (1 P)
1 fruit (1 C)	1 fruit (1 C)
6 almonds (1 F)	Broccoli sprouts
¼ cup low-fat cottage cheese (1 P)	**Snack**
	12 ounces low-sodium V8 juice (1 C)
Dinner	**Dinner**
3 ounces shrimp (3 P) sautéed with 1 Tbsp. olive oil (1 F) and 3 cups non-starchy vegetables (2 C)	3 ounces shrimp or scallops, broiled (3 P)
	2 ½ cups green vegetables and ½ cup diced tomatoes (2 C)
Snack	**Snack**
Sugar-free Jell-O (free)	1 fruits (1 C)
1 fruit (1 C)	10 peanuts (1 F)

It's time for your weekly weigh-in. See how much you've already accomplished!

Day Nine	**Day Ten**
Breakfast	**Breakfast**
1 cup *Good Friends* and ½ cup skim milk (2 C)	1 fruit (1 C)
1 fruit (1 C)	1 cup cooked oatmeal made with water (2 C)
Lunch	Cinnamon
2 slices whole-wheat bread (2 C)	**Lunch**
1 cup grilled tofu (2 P)	2 slices rye bread (2 C)
1/3 cup Hummus *recipe* (1 C) (1 P)	2 ounces tuna (2 P)
Broccoli sprouts	1 Tbsp. light mayonnaise (1 F)
Snack	Lettuce and broccoli sprouts and tomato
1 fruit (1 C)	**Snack**
6 almonds (1 F)	1 low-fat yogurt 6 oz. (1 C) (1 P)
Dinner	¾ cup Kashi's *Good Friends* cereal (1 C)
Salad with 1 tsp. olive oil plus vinegar (1 F)	2 walnuts (1 F)
1 ½ cups green vegetables (1 C)	**Dinner**
4 ounces grilled fish (4 P)	*Dining out*:
Snack	Caesar salad with no croutons, and dressing on the side (1 C) (1 P) (2 F)
30 peanuts (3 F)	3 ounces grilled fish or poultry (3 P)
25-calorie fat-free hot cocoa (free)	**Snack**
	Sugar-free Jell-O (free)

Have you tried any new foods? Low-sodium V8 or tomato juice works wonders to fill up your stomach!

Day Eleven
Breakfast
3/4 cup high-fiber cereal (5 grams of fiber or more) (1 C)
½ cup skim milk and ½ fruit serving (1 C)
2 walnuts, chopped (1 F)
Lunch
6 " *Subway* sandwich (3 C) no cheese
2 Tbsp. light dressing or 1 Tbsp. light mayonnaise (1 F)
2 ounces turkey, teriyaki chicken, seafood salad, tuna (already has mayonnaise) or garden burger (2 P)
Snack
12 ounces low-sodium V8 or tomato juice (1 C)
Dinner
5 ounces fish, poultry, or boneless pork tenderloin (5 P)
1 ½ cups vegetables (1 C)
Snack
18 cashews (3 F)
1 fruit (1 C)

Day Twelve
Breakfast
1 cup *Wheatena* made with water (2 C)
2 walnuts, chopped (1 F)
Cinnamon
Lunch
1 large slice pizza plain or with vegetables (2 C) (2 P) (2 F)
Snack
1 fruit (1 C)
6 cashews (1 F)
Dinner
4 ounces fish, poultry, or lean meat (4 P)
3 cups vegetables (2 C)
1 slice low-fat cheese melted on top (1 P)
Snack
1 fruit (1 C)
6 almonds (1 F)

Have you been using low-fat milk in your coffee?

Day Thirteen	**_Day Fourteen_**
Breakfast	**Breakfast**
¾ cup high-fiber cereal (1 C)	½ large pumpernickel bagel
½ cup low fat milk and ½ fruit	(2 C)
serving (1 C)	1 Tbsp. light whipped butter
Lunch	(1 F)
Large salad (1 C)	**Lunch**
Broccoli sprouts	Large salad (1 C)
2 ounces tuna (2 P)	Broccoli sprouts
2 Tbsp. light dressing (1 F)	3 ounces baked salmon (3 P)
½ cup chickpeas (1 C) (1 P)	2 Tbsp. light dressing (1 F)
Snack	**Snack**
1 fruit (1 C)	1 fruit (1 C)
6 almonds (1 F)	6 almonds (1 F)
Dinner	**Dinner**
4 ounces chicken (4 P),	4 ounces fish, grilled (4 P),
sautéed with 2 tsp. olive oil	sautéed with 2 tsp. olive oil
(2 F) and 3 cups non-starchy	(2 F) and 3 cups non-starchy
vegetables (2 C)	vegetables (2 C)
Snack	**Snack**
1 fruit (1 C)	Sugar-free Jell-O (free)
6 cashews (1 F)	2 fruits (2 C)
25-calorie *fat-free hot cocoa* (free)	

It's time for your weekly weigh-in. See how much you've already accomplished!

Have you lost weight during these first two weeks? If not, review the rules and start from Day One! You can do it!

Be sure to drink your water daily!

STELLA

<u>*Regular eating patterns – for life!*</u>

<u>Day Fifteen</u>	<u>Day Sixteen</u>
Breakfast	**Breakfast**
1 slice whole-grain bread (1 C)	High-Fiber Muffin *recipe*
¼ cup low-fat cottage cheese	(1 C) (1 F)
(1 P) with cinnamon melted on	**Lunch**
top	Marinated Bean and Vegetable
Lunch	Salad *recipe* (1 C) (1 P) (2 F)
2 slices pumpernickel bread	**Snack**
(2 C)	1 fruit (1 C)
3 ounces turkey (3 P)	6 almonds (1 F)
Lettuce and tomato	**Dinner**
Snack	4 ounces flounder, baked (4 P)
6 crackers (1 C)	1 tsp. olive oil to stir fry (1 F):
Eggplant Caponata á la Lois	1 cup black beans (2 C) (2 P)
recipe (3 F) (1 C)	1 ½ cups non-starchy
Dinner	vegetables (1 C)
Scallops and Broccoli *recipe*	**Snack**
(3 P) (1 C) (1 F)	2 fruits (2 C)
2/3 cup cooked whole-wheat	
pasta (2 C)	
Snack	
Sugar-free Jell-O (free)	
25-calorie fat-free hot cocoa	
(free)	
10 peanuts (1 F)	

Deserve.
You deserve to be happy. Overindulgence in food doesn't make you happy; it gives you a temporary feeling of pleasure. Be your happiest by reaching your goals!

Day Seventeen	***Day Eighteen***
Breakfast	**Breakfast**
1 cup cooked oatmeal made with water (2 C)	¾ cup high-fiber cereal (1 C)
2 Tbsp. flaxseed meal, unprocessed oat bran, or unprocessed bran (1 C)	½ cup low-fat milk and ½ fruit serving (1 C)
1 fruit (1 C)	**Lunch**
Lunch	Small salad
1 light fruit yogurt (1 C) (1 P)	2 Tbsp. light dressing (1 F)
12 cashews (2 F)	10 low-sodium black olives (1 F)
Snack	3 ounces baked chicken (3 P)
12 ounces of low-sodium V8 juice (1 C)	**Snack**
Dinner	15 baked tortilla chips (1 C)
Poached Salmon *recipe* (6 P)	1 serving Black Bean and Corn Dip (2 C) (1 P)
Brussels sprouts *recipe* (2 F) (½ C)	**Dinner**
Snack	3 ounces grilled salmon (3 P)
1 large baked apple made with cinnamon (1 ½ C)	1 cup cooked kasha (2 C)
2 walnuts (1 F)	1 ½ cups green vegetables (1C)
	Snack
	18 cashews (3 F)
	25-calorie fat-free hot cocoa (free)

Have you tried to consume your food more slowly?

Day Nineteen	*Day Twenty*
Breakfast	**Breakfast**
High-fiber muffin (1 C) (1 F)	Oat Bran Flaxseed Muffin *recipe* (2 C) (1 F)
Lunch	**Lunch**
2 slices bread (2 C)	2 slices whole-wheat pita bread (2 C)
2 ounces turkey (2 P)	1 cup grilled tofu (2 P)
Lettuce and tomato	Hummus *recipe* (1 C) (1 P)
Snack	Lettuce, tomatoes, sprouts
Eggplant Dip *recipe* (1 C) (1 F)	**Snack**
Served with 6 crackers and 1 cup vegetables (1 C)	Low-Fat Spinach *recipe* (1 C)
Dinner	1 cup vegetables to dip (free)
Shrimp, Tomato, Spinach and Feta *recipe* (4 P) (1 F) (1 C)	**Dinner**
Bulgur Pilaf *recipe* (1 C) (1 F)	4 ounces salmon (4 P)
Snack	Cauliflower Casserole *recipe* (1 C) (1 F)
1 light fruit yogurt 6 oz. (1 C) (1 P)	**Snack**
6 cashews (1 F)	1 fruit (1 C)
	12 almonds (2 F)
	6 cashews (1 F)

Energy.
Eating high-fiber foods or combining carbohydrates with lean protein or monounsaturated fats will help to diminish hunger, and will sustain your energy level.

Day Twenty-One **Breakfast** 1 cup cooked oatmeal made with water (2 C) 2 walnuts, chopped (1 F) Cinnamon **Lunch** 1 light fruit yogurt (1 C) (1 P) ¾ cup Kashi's *Good Friends* cereal (1 C) 6 almonds (1 F) 2 walnuts (1 F) **Snack** Low-Fat Spinach Dip *recipe* (1 C) 1 cup vegetables to dip **Dinner** Salmon Teriyaki, Kasha and Vegetables *recipe* (6 P) (3 C) **Snack** Sugar-free Jell-O (free) 12 cashews (2 F)	***Day Twenty-Two*** **Breakfast** 1 slice toast (1 C) ¼ cup low-fat cottage cheese (1 P) Melt with cinnamon **Lunch** Small salad 2 tsp. olive oil plus vinegar (2 F) 1 ounce goat cheese (1 P) 3 ounces poultry or fish (3 P) **Snack** *Alba 70* shake made with ½ cup milk and ½ cup water or Fruit shake: *¾ cup berries, 4 ounces skim milk, ½ ripe banana and ice (2 C)* **Dinner** 1 hamburger bun (2 C) 1-Vegetable Burger (2 P) 6-ounce medium potato (baked as fries) *recipe* (2 C) Homemade Coleslaw *recipe* (1 F) **Snack** 1 fruit (1 C) 12 almonds (2 F)

It's time for your weekly weigh-in. See how much you've already accomplished!

<u>**Day Twenty-Three**</u>	<u>**Day Twenty-Four**</u>
Breakfast	**Breakfast**
High-fiber muffin *recipe* (1 C) (1 F)	1 whole-wheat English muffin (2 C)
Lunch	1 Tbsp. light whipped butter (1 F)
Portabella Mushroom Sandwich *recipe* (1 C) (2 P)	**Lunch**
Snack	½ small cantaloupe (2 C)
6 animal crackers (1 C) 25-calorie fat-free hot cocoa (free)	½ cup low-fat cottage cheese (2 P)
Dinner	**Snack**
Eggplant Lasagna *recipe* (2 C) (4 P)	6 vanilla wafers (1 C) 25-calorie fat-free hot cocoa (free)
Snack	**Dinner**
1 cup low-fat ice cream (2 C) (1 P) (1 F) ¼ cup granola (1 C) 6 walnuts (3 F)	4 ounces grilled salmon (4 P) Potato-Zucchini Cake *recipe* (1 P) (2 C) (2 F)
	Snack
	½ cup low-fat ice cream (1 C) 4 walnuts (2 F)

Freedom.
Making the right food choices can be liberating! Make food a positive factor in your life! Don't abuse it!

Day Twenty-Five	**_Day Twenty-Six_**
Breakfast	**Breakfast**
1 cup Kashi's *Good Friends* cereal and ½ cup skim milk (2 C)	1 fruit (1 C) ½ cup cottage cheese (2 P)
Lunch	**Lunch**
Garden burger (2 P) 1 hamburger bun (2 C) Broccoli sprouts 2 Tbsp. avocado (1 F)	Vegetable Soup *recipe* and 30 oyster crackers (2 C)
Snack	**Snack**
1 fruit (1 C) 12 cashews (2 F)	3 – 4 cups popcorn (1 C)
Dinner	**Dinner**
5 ounces grilled chicken (5 P) 1 medium 6-oz. sweet potato (baked as chips) *recipe* (2 C)	5 ounces fish, poultry, or lean meat, baked (5 P) Tabouleh *recipe* (1 C) (1 F) 1 ½ cups steamed broccoli (1C) 6 almonds slivered on broccoli (1 F)
Snack	**Snack**
½ cup vanilla fat-free yogurt and ¼ cup Kashi's *Good Friends* cereal (1 C) 6 almonds and 2 walnuts (2 F)	½ cup vanilla fat-free yogurt and ¼ cup Kashi's *Good Friends* cereal (1 C) 1 fruit (1 C) 6 walnuts (3 F)

How is exercise making you feel? Remember you should progress to 45 minutes of exercise at least 5 times a week. Combine resistance training with your cardiovascular workout.

<u>**Day Twenty-Seven**</u>	<u>**Day Twenty-Eight**</u>
Breakfast 2-egg omelet (2 P) (2 F) 1 tsp. canola oil (to make omelet) (1 F) Tomatoes and spinach (free) 1 slice low-fat cheese (1 P) **Lunch** Small salad with 2 Tbsp. light dressing (1 F) 3 ounces of fish, chicken, lean meat (3 P) **Snack** ¾ cup Kashi's *Good Friends* cereal (1 C) 3 dried apricots (1 C) 6 pistachio nuts (1 F) **Dinner** Eggplant Parmigiana Hero (5 C) 1 slice low-fat cheese (1 P) **Snack** 1 crepe, ½ banana and ¼ cup berries (1 C) 2 Tbsp. light whipped cream (free)	**Breakfast** 1 whole-wheat English muffin (2 C) 2 slices Jarlsberg light cheese (2 P) 2 slices of tomato **Lunch** Spinach Pie *recipe* (2 P) (1 C) (1F) **Snack** 12 ounces of low-sodium V8 or tomato juice (1 C) **Dinner** Shrimp, Vegetable, and Pasta Casserole *recipe* (2C) (3 P) (2 F) **Snack** 12 almonds (2 F) 2 fruits (2 C)

It's time for your weekly weigh-in. See how much you've already accomplished!

### *Day Twenty-Nine* **Breakfast** ¼ cup low-fat cottage cheese (1 P) 1 slice whole-grain bread (1 C) **Lunch** Small salad with 2 Tbsp. light dressing (1 F) 3 ounces shrimp (3 P) 10 peanuts (1 F) **Snack** 12 ounces low-sodium V8 or tomato juice (1 C) **Dinner** Vegetable Chow Mein *recipe* (2 C) (1 F) Add 3 ounces of chicken or shrimp (3 P) **Snack** 2 Applesauce-Oatmeal Cookies *recipe* (4 C) (2 F) 25-calorie fat-free hot cocoa (free)	### *Day Thirty* **Breakfast** Fruit shake: blend 1 ripe banana with ¾ cup berries and 8 ounces low-fat milk (3 C) (1 P) **Lunch** Small salad with 2 Tbsp. light dressing (1 F) 3 ounces chicken, baked (3 P) **Snack** 1 light fruit yogurt (1 C) (1 P) 6 almonds (1 F) **Dinner** Veggie Mexican *recipe* (3 C) (2 P) (1 F) **Snack** 12 cashews (2 F) 1 fruit (1 C) Sugar-free Jell-O (free)

Go for it! Get ready for a lifetime of success. There's nothing but YOU to stop you from having what you want. Be the strong, accomplished person you know you can be.

Marci's 1400-Mile Journey
Sample Daily Tracker

1400 Miles	Carbohydrate: 9 servings	Protein: 9 servings	Fat: 6 servings

You are allowed the following amounts of carbohydrates, proteins and fats. Choose them wisely! Check off the boxes as you consume each serving.

C=Carbohydrates (starch, fruit, milk, vegetables): 1 serving has 15 grams of total carbohydrate. Pick 9 servings. Refer to food serving size list.

15 g	15 g	15 g	15 g	15 g
15 g	15 g	15 g	15 g	XXXXXX

P=Proteins (fish, poultry, meat, eggs, cheese, tofu, etc.): Choose mostly very lean or lean. 1 serving has 7 grams of protein or 1 ounce. Pick 9 servings.

7 g	7 g	7 g	7 g	7 g
7 g	7 g	7 g	7 g	XXXXXXX

F=Fats (oils, nuts, butters, etc.): Choose mostly monounsaturated fats. 1 serving has 5 grams of fat. Pick 6 servings.

5g	5 g	5 g	5 g	5 g	5 g

W=Water

16 ounces	16 ounces	16 ounces	16 ounces

Marci's 1400-Mile Weekly Tracker

DAY 1	C	C	C	C	C	C	C	C	C
	P	P	P	P	P	P	P	P	P
	F	F	F	F	F	F			
DAY 2	C	C	C	C	C	C	C	C	C
	P	P	P	P	P	P	P	P	P
	F	F	F	F	F	F			
DAY 3	C	C	C	C	C	C	C	C	C
	P	P	P	P	P	P	P	P	P
	F	F	F	F	F	F			
DAY 4	C	C	C	C	C	C	C	C	C
	P	P	P	P	P	P	P	P	P
	F	F	F	F	F	F			
DAY 5	C	C	C	C	C	C	C	C	C
	P	P	P	P	P	P	P	P	P
	F	F	F	F	F	F			
DAY 6	C	C	C	C	C	C	C	C	C
	P	P	P	P	P	P	P	P	P
	F	F	F	F	F	F			
DAY 7	C	C	C	C	C	C	C	C	C
	P	P	P	P	P	P	P	P	P
	F	F	F	F	F	F			

Have you tried mixing red raspberry herbal iced tea with 2 ounces of cran-raspberry juice to sweeten it?

Marci's 1400-Mile Weekly Tracker

DAY 1	C	C	C	C	C	C	C	C	C
	P	P	P	P	P	P	P	P	P
	F	F	F	F	F	F			
DAY 2	C	C	C	C	C	C	C	C	C
	P	P	P	P	P	P	P	P	P
	F	F	F	F	F	F			
DAY 3	C	C	C	C	C	C	C	C	C
	P	P	P	P	P	P	P	P	P
	F	F	F	F	F	F			
DAY 4	C	C	C	C	C	C	C	C	C
	P	P	P	P	P	P	P	P	P
	F	F	F	F	F	F			
DAY 5	C	C	C	C	C	C	C	C	C
	P	P	P	P	P	P	P	P	P
	F	F	F	F	F	F			
DAY 6	C	C	C	C	C	C	C	C	C
	P	P	P	P	P	P	P	P	P
	F	F	F	F	F	F			
DAY 7	C	C	C	C	C	C	C	C	C
	P	P	P	P	P	P	P	P	P
	F	F	F	F	F	F			

Try to focus on gradually increasing your fiber intake to 30-50 grams each day!

Marci's 1400-Mile Weekly Tracker

DAY 1	C	C	C	C	C	C	C	C	C
	P	P	P	P	P	P	P	P	P
	F	F	F	F	F	F			
DAY 2	C	C	C	C	C	C	C	C	C
	P	P	P	P	P	P	P	P	P
	F	F	F	F	F	F			
DAY 3	C	C	C	C	C	C	C	C	C
	P	P	P	P	P	P	P	P	P
	F	F	F	F	F	F			
DAY 4	C	C	C	C	C	C	C	C	C
	P	P	P	P	P	P	P	P	P
	F	F	F	F	F	F			
DAY 5	C	C	C	C	C	C	C	C	C
	P	P	P	P	P	P	P	P	P
	F	F	F	F	F	F			
DAY 6	C	C	C	C	C	C	C	C	C
	P	P	P	P	P	P	P	P	P
	F	F	F	F	F	F			
DAY 7	C	C	C	C	C	C	C	C	C
	P	P	P	P	P	P	P	P	P
	F	F	F	F	F	F			

Heal yourself.
Healthy eating makes you feel good
about yourself. It even tastes good and
the food is easy to prepare as well.

Marci's 1400-Mile Weekly Tracker

DAY 1	C	C	C	C	C	C	C	C	C
	P	P	P	P	P	P	P	P	P
	F	F	F	F	F	F			
DAY 2	C	C	C	C	C	C	C	C	C
	P	P	P	P	P	P	P	P	P
	F	F	F	F	F	F			
DAY 3	C	C	C	C	C	C	C	C	C
	P	P	P	P	P	P	P	P	P
	F	F	F	F	F	F			
DAY 4	C	C	C	C	C	C	C	C	C
	P	P	P	P	P	P	P	P	P
	F	F	F	F	F	F			
DAY 5	C	C	C	C	C	C	C	C	C
	P	P	P	P	P	P	P	P	P
	F	F	F	F	F	F			
DAY 6	C	C	C	C	C	C	C	C	C
	P	P	P	P	P	P	P	P	P
	F	F	F	F	F	F			
DAY 7	C	C	C	C	C	C	C	C	C
	P	P	P	P	P	P	P	P	P
	F	F	F	F	F	F			

*Eating fruits and vegetables add water
and fiber to your healthy day!*

Marci's 1400-Mile 2-Week Shortcut

Day One	*Day Two*
Breakfast	**Breakfast**
1 whole-wheat English muffin (2 C)	1 cup cooked oatmeal made with water (2 C)
2 ounces goat cheese (2 P)	1 Fuit (1 C)
Lunch	2 walnuts, chopped (1 F)
Large salad (1 C)	Cinnamon
3 ounces tuna (3 P)	**Lunch**
2 Tbsp. light dressing (1 F)	2 slices whole-wheat bread (2 C)
10 peanuts (1 F)	3 ounces turkey, tuna (3 P)
½ cup chickpeas (1 C) (1 P)	Mustard
Snack	**Snack**
1 fruit (1 C)	Baked apple (1 C)
12 almonds (2 F)	4 walnuts, chopped (2 F)
Dinner	**Dinner**
1 large bowl Veggie Soup *recipe* (1C)	Salad with 2 tsp. olive oil plus vinegar (2 F)
3 ounces shrimp, grilled with spices (3 P)	1 cup broccoli, steamed with ½ cup no-salt canned diced tomatoes (1 C)
1 cup cooked spinach with ½ cup no-salt diced tomatoes (1 C)	6 ounces salmon, grilled with garlic and 1 Tbsp. of light teriyaki sauce (6 P)
Snack	**Snack**
12 almonds (2 F)	2 fruit (2 C)
2 fruits (2 C)	6 almonds, slivered (1 F)

Today is your first day! Make sure to weigh yourself so you will see your results!

Day Three

Breakfast
1 cup cooked *Wheatena* (2 C)
1 fruit (1 C)
4 walnuts, chopped (2 F)
Cinnamon

Lunch
Caesar Salad *recipe*
(1 C) (1 P) (2 F)
Add 4 ounces shrimp (4 P)

Snack
12 ounces low-sodium V8 or
tomato juice (1 C)

Dinner
Large bowl of Veggie Soup
recipe (1 C)
4 ounces of chicken (4 P)
Large Salad (1 C)
2 Tbsp. light dressing (1 F)

Snack
2 fruits (2 C)
6 cashews (1 F)

Day Four

Breakfast
1 slice whole-grain bread (1 C)
½ cup fat-free or 1% cottage
cheese (2 P)
1 cup fresh fruit (1 C)

Lunch
2 slices rye bread (2 C)
2 slices low-fat cheese (2 P)
2 slices tomato

Snack
3-4 cups of popcorn (1 C)

Dinner
Salad with 2 Tbsp. light
dressing (1 F)
10 low-sodium black olives (1 F)
5 ounces fish or poultry
(5 P) grilled with spices
3 cups broccoli (2 C)
1 tsp. olive oil drizzled on top of
vegetables (1 F)
6 almonds (1 F)

Snack
2 fruits (2 C)
12 almonds (2 F)

I am worth it.
So I can do it! I will be healthy and feel
great while I enjoy the food I am eating.

Day Five

Breakfast

1 English muffin (2 C)
1 egg fried in *Pam* spray
(1 P) (1 F)
1 slice low-fat cheese (1 P)

Lunch

2 slices whole-wheat bread
(2 C)
2 ounces shrimp or chicken
salad (2 P)
1 Tbsp. light mayonnaise (for
salad) (1 F)

Snack

1 light fruit yogurt (1 C) (1 P)
6 almonds (1 F)

Dinner

1 Tbsp. olive oil (3 F) to sauté 3
cups vegetables (2 C)
4 ounces fish, poultry, or lean
meat (4 P)

Snack

Sugar-free Jell-O (free)
2 fruits (2 C)
25-calorie fat-free hot cocoa
(free)

Day Six

Breakfast

2 frozen *Go Lean* low-fat,
whole-grain waffles (2 C)
2 Tbsp. maple syrup (2 C)

Lunch

Large salad (1 C)
3 ounces chicken (3 P)
10 peanuts (1 F)
1 Tbsp. olive oil plus vinegar
(3 F)

Snack

1 cup carrots and celery (free)

Dinner

3 cups vegetables steamed
with 2 Tbsp. salsa (2 C)
4 ounces shrimp grilled or
baked with spices (4 P)
2 slices low-fat shredded
cheese melted on top (2 P)

Snack

¾ cup Kashi's *Good Friends*
cereal (1 C)
3 dried apricots (1 C)
12 cashews (2 F)

*Consuming vegetable soup will fill you up
with few calories and many nutrients!*

Day Seven	**_Day Eight_**
Breakfast	**Breakfast**
1 cup cooked oatmeal made with water (2 C)	2 slices bread (2 C)
1 small banana (1 C)	2 slice low-fat cheese (2 P)
2 walnuts, chopped (1 F)	2 eggs poached (2 P) (2 F)
Lunch	**Lunch**
Avocado, Shrimp, Roasted Garlic and Walnut salad *recipe* (1 C) (3 P) (3 F)	Large salad (1 C)
	Vinaigrette Dressing *recipe* (2 F)
Snack	½ cup grilled tofu (1 P)
1 fruit (1 C)	1 fruit (1 C)
6 almonds (1 F)	**Snack**
½ cup low fat cottage cheese (2 P)	12 ounces low-sodium V8 juice (1 C)
Dinner	**Dinner**
4 ounces shrimp (4 P) sautéed with 1 Tbsp. olive oil (1 F) and 3 cups non-starchy vegetables (2 C)	4 ounces scallops broiled (4 P)
	2 ½ cups green vegetables and ½ cup diced tomatoes (2 C)
Snack	**Snack**
Sugar-free Jell-O (free)	2 fruits (2 C)
2 fruits (2 C)	20 peanuts (2 F)

It's time for your weekly weigh-in. See how much you've already accomplished!

Day Nine

Breakfast
1 cup *Good Friends* and
½ cup skim milk (2 C)
1 fruit (1 C)

Lunch
2 slices whole-wheat bread
(2 C)
1 cup grilled tofu (2 P)
1/3 cup Hummus *recipe*
(1 C) (1 P)
Broccoli sprouts

Snack
1 light fruit yogurt (1 C) (1 P)
12 almonds (2 F)

Dinner
Salad with 1 tsp. olive oil plus
vinegar (1 F)
1 ½ cups green vegetables
(1 C)
5 ounces grilled fish (5 P)

Snack
30 peanuts (3 F)
1 fruit (1 C)
25-calorie fat-free hot cocoa
(free)

Day Ten

Breakfast
1 fruit (1 C)
1 cup cooked oatmeal made
with water (2 C)
2 walnuts, chopped (1 F)
Cinnamon

Lunch
2 slices rye bread (2 C)
3 ounces tuna (3 P)
1 Tbsp. light mayonnaise (1 F)
Lettuce and tomato

Snack
1 low-fat yogurt 6 oz. (1 C) (1 P)
¾ cup Kashi's *Good Friends*
cereal (1 C)
2 walnuts (1 F)

Dinner
Dining out:
Caesar salad with no croutons,
and dressing on the side
(1 C) (3 F)
5 ounces grilled fish or poultry
(5 P)

Snack
1 fruit (1 C)
Sugar-free Jell-O (free)

Try 25-calorie fat-free hot cocoa with 2 Tbsp.
of light whipped cream for a delicous treat.

Day Eleven	Day Twelve
Breakfast	**Breakfast**
3/4 cup high-fiber cereal (5 grams of fiber or more) (1 C) ½ cup skim milk and ½ fruit serving (1 C) 4 walnuts, chopped (2 F)	1 cup *Wheatena* made with water (2 C) 2 walnuts, chopped (1 F) Cinnamon
Lunch	**Lunch**
6" Subway sandwich (3 C) no cheese 2 Tbsp. light dressing or 1 Tbsp. light mayonnaise (1 F) 2 ounces turkey, teriyaki chicken, seafood salad, tuna (already has mayonnaise) or garden burger (2 P)	1 large slice pizza plain or with vegetables (2 C) (2 P) (2 F)
Snack	**Snack**
12 ounces low-sodium V8 or tomato juice (1 C)	1 fruit (1 C) 6 cashews (1 F)
Dinner	**Dinner**
5 ounces boneless pork tenderloin (5 P) 3 cups vegetables (2 C) 2 ounces low-fat shredded cheese (2 P)	6 ounces fish, poultry, or lean meat (6 P) 3 cups vegetables (2 C) 1 slice low-fat cheese melted on top (1 P)
Snack	**Snack**
18 cashews (3 F) 1 fruit (1 C)	2 fruits (2 C) 12 almonds (2 F)

Have you seen your doctor for blood work? Blood tests can show you the positive outcomes of your actions.

<u>*Day Thirteen*</u> **Breakfast** ¾ cup high-fiber cereal (1 C) ½ cup low-fat milk and ½ fruit serving (1 C) **Lunch** Large salad (1 C) 2 ounces tuna (2 P) 2 Tbsp. light dressing (1 F) ½ cup chickpeas (1 C) (1 P) **Snack** 1 fruit (1 C) 6 almonds (1 F) **Dinner** 6 ounces chicken (6 P), sautéed with 2 tsp. olive oil (2 F) 3 cups non-starchy vegetables (2 C) **Snack** 2 fruits (2 C) 12 cashews (2 F) 25-calorie fat-free hot cocoa (free)	**<u>*Day Fourteen*</u>** **Breakfast** ½ large pumpernickel bagel (2 C) 1 poached egg (1 P) (1 F) 1 Tbsp. light whipped butter (1 F) 1 slice tomato **Lunch** Large salad (1 C) 3 ounces baked salmon (3 P) ½ cup chick peas (1 C) (1 P) 2 Tbsp. light dressing (1 F) **Snack** 1 fruit (1 C) 6 almonds (1 F) **Dinner** 4 ounces fish, grilled (4 P) 3 cups non-starchy vegetables (2 C), sautéed with 2 tsp. olive oil (2 F) **Snack** Sugar-free Jell-O (free) 2 fruits (2 C)

It's time for your weekly weigh-in. See how much you've already accomplished!

Have you lost weight during these first two weeks? If not review the rules and start from Day One! You can do it!

Be sure to drink your water daily!

MARCI

Regular eating patterns – for life!

Day Fifteen	*Day Sixteen*
Breakfast 2 slices whole-grain bread (2 C) ½ cup low-fat cottage cheese (2 P) with cinnamon melted on top	**Breakfast** High-Fiber Muffin *recipe* (1 C) (1 F)
Lunch 2 slices pumpernickel bread (2 C) 3 ounces turkey (3 P) 1 slice low-fat cheese (1 P) Lettuce and tomato	**Lunch** Marinated Bean and Vegetable Salad *recipe* (1 C) (1 P) (2 F)
Snack 6 crackers (1 C) Eggplant Caponata á la Lois *recipe* (3 F) (1 C)	**Snack** 12 ounces of low sodium V8 juice (1 C)
Dinner Scallops and Broccoli *recipe* (3 P) (1 C) (1 F) 2/3 cup cooked whole-wheat pasta (2 C)	**Dinner** 6 ounces flounder, baked (6 P) 1 Tbsp. olive oil to stir fry (3 F): 1 cup black beans (2 C) (2 P) 3 cups non-starchy vegetables (2 C)
Snack Sugar-free Jell-O (free) 25 calorie fat-free hot cocoa (free) 20 peanuts (2 F)	**Snack** 2 fruits (2 C)

Join me: Be a winner of The Diet Game! You will achieve permanent weight loss. You will work hard for the results, but you will reap all the benefits.

Day Seventeen	*Day Eighteen*
Breakfast	**Breakfast**
1 cup cooked oatmeal made with water (2 C)	¾ cup high-fiber cereal (1 C)
4 walnuts (2 F)	½ cup low-fat milk and ½ fruit serving (1 C)
2 Tbsp. flaxseed meal, unprocessed oat bran, or unprocessed bran (1 C)	**Lunch**
1 fruit (1 C)	Large salad (1 C)
Lunch	2 Tbsp. light dressing (1 F)
2 slices whole-grain bread (2 C)	10 low-sodium black olives (1 F)
3 ounces tuna (3 P)	2 ounces baked chicken (2 P)
1 Tbsp. light mayonnaise (1 F)	1 hard-boiled egg (1 P) (1 F)
Snack	**Snack**
12 ounces of low-sodium V8 juice (1 C)	15 baked tortilla chips (1 C)
Dinner	1 serving Black Bean and Corn Dip (2 C) (1 P)
Poached salmon *recipe* (6 P)	**Dinner**
Brussels sprouts *recipe* (2 F) (½ C)	5 ounces grilled salmon (5 P)
Snack	1 cup cooked kasha (2 C)
1 large baked apple made with cinnamon (1 ½ C)	1 ½ cups green vegetables (1 C)
2 walnuts (1 F)	**Snack**
	18 cashews (3 F)

Be careful not to buy fat-free foods before checking out the calories and increased amounts of sugar or carbohydrates. Be aware that low carbohydrate foods may have high amounts of saturated fat so watch out!

<u>Day Nineteen</u> **Breakfast** High-fiber muffin *recipe* (1 C) (1 F) **Lunch** 2 slices bread (2 C) 3 ounces turkey (3 P) 1 slice low-fat cheese (1 P) Lettuce and tomato 1 fruit (1 C) **Snack** Eggplant Dip *recipe* (1 C) (1 F) Served with 6 crackers and 1 cup vegetables (1 C) **Dinner** Shrimp, Tomato, Spinach and Feta *recipe* (4 P) (1 F) (1 C) Bulgur Pilaf *recipe* (1 C) (1 F) **Snack** 1 light fruit yogurt 6 oz. (1 C) (1 P) 12 cashews (2 F)	**<u>Day Twenty</u>** **Breakfast** Oat bran Flaxseed Muffin *recipe* (2 C) (1 F) **Lunch** 2 slices whole-wheat pita bread (2 C) 1 cup grilled tofu (2 P) Hummus *recipe* (1 C) (1 P) 2 Tbsp. avocado (1 F) Lettuce, tomatoes, sprouts **Snack** Low-fat spinach *recipe* (1 C) 1 cup vegetables to dip **Dinner** Fried Flounder *recipe* (6 P) (1 C) Cauliflower Casserole *recipe* (1 C) (1 F) **Snack** 1 fruit (1 C) 18 almonds (3 F)

Try to eat fruits and vegetables for your snacks. One fruit has 60 calories, 12 ounces of V8 juice has 75 calories and 3 cups of raw vegetables has 75 calories. 22 small pretzels have 110 calories and 1 small scoop of low-fat ice cream has 100 calories!! (Who can stop at that?)

Day Twenty-One	*Day Twenty-Two*
Breakfast	**Breakfast**
1 cup cooked oatmeal made with water (2 C)	1 slice toast (1 C)
4 walnuts, chopped (2 F)	½ cup low-fat cottage cheese (2 P)
Cinnamon	**Lunch**
Lunch	Large salad (1 C)
Large salad (1 C)	2 tsp. olive oil plus vinegar (2 F)
½ cup chick peas (1 C) (1 P)	10 peanuts (1 F)
2 ounces shrimp (2 P)	2 ounces goat cheese (2 P)
10 low-sodium olives (1 F)	3 ounces poultry or fish (3 P)
2 Tbsp. light dressing (1 F)	**Snack**
Snack	*Alba 70* shake made with ½ cup milk and ½ cup water or
Low-fat spinach dip *recipe* (1 C)	Fruit shake *¾ cup berries,*
1 cup vegetables to dip	*4 ounces skim milk, ½ ripe*
Dinner	*banana and ice (2 C)*
Salmon Teriyaki, Kasha and Vegetables *recipe* (6 P) (3 C)	**Dinner**
Snack	1 hamburger bun (2 C)
Sugar-free Jell-O (free)	1 Vegetable Burger (2 P)
1 fruit (1 C)	6-ounce medium potato (baked as fries) *recipe* (2 C)
12 cashews (2 F)	Homemade coleslaw *recipe* (1 F)
	Snack
	1 fruit (1 C)
	12 almonds (2 F)

It's time to weigh in. See how much you've already accomplished!

Day Twenty-Three	_Day Twenty-Four_
Breakfast	**Breakfast**
High-fiber muffin *recipe* (1 C) (1 F)	1 whole-wheat English muffin (2 C)
Lunch	1 poached egg (1 P) (1 F)
Portabella Mushroom Sandwich *recipe* (1 C) (2 P)	1 Tbsp. light whipped butter (1 F)
Snack	**Lunch**
8 animal crackers (1 C)	½ small cantaloupe (2 C)
25-calorie fat-free hot cocoa (free)	½ cup low-fat cottage cheese (2 P)
Dinner	**Snack**
6 ounces grilled fish (6 P)	6 vanilla wafers (1 C)
2 tsp. olive oil (2 F)	25-calorie fat-free hot cocoa (free)
1 cup cooked kasha (2 C)	**Dinner**
1 ½ cups cooked broccoli (1 C)	4 ounces grilled salmon (4 P)
Snack	Potato-Zucchini Cake *recipe* (1 P) (2 C) (2 F)
1 cup low-fat ice cream (2 C) (1 P) (1 F)	**Snack**
¼ cup granola (1 C)	1 cup low-fat ice cream (2 C) (1 P)
4 walnuts (2 F)	4 walnuts (2 F)

Keep an open mind. It can be a bit of a struggle at first, but you CAN do it!

Day Twenty-Five

Breakfast
1 cup Kashi's *Good Friends* cereal and
½ cup skim milk (2 C)

Lunch
Garden burger (2 P)
1 slice low-fat cheese (1 P)
1 hamburger bun (2 C)
Broccoli sprouts
2 Tbsp. avocado (1 F)

Snack
1 fruit (1 C)
12 cashews (2 F)

Dinner
6 ounces grilled chicken (6 P)
1 medium 6-oz. sweet potato (baked as chips) *recipe* (2 C)
1 ½ cups vegetables, steamed (1 C)

Snack
½ cup vanilla fat-free yogurt and ¼ cup Kashi's *Good Friends* cereal (1 C)
12 almonds and 2 walnuts (3 F)

Day Twenty-Six

Breakfast
1 fruit (1 C)
½ cup cottage cheese (2 P)

Lunch
Vegetable Soup *recipe* (1 C)
½ sandwich with 1 slice bread (1 C)
1 egg (1 P) (1 F)
1 slice tomato

Snack
6 – 8 cups popcorn (2 C)

Dinner
5 ounces fish, poultry, or lean meat, baked (5 P)
Tabouleh *recipe* (1 C) (1 F)
1 ½ cups steamed broccoli (1 C)
6 almonds slivered on broccoli (1 F)

Snack
1 cup low-fat ice cream (2 C) (1 P)
6 walnuts (3 F)

Buy foods that are already portioned. If you buy an ice pop instead of a pint of ice cream your portions will be more controlled.

Day Twenty-Seven

Breakfast
2-egg omelet (2 P) (2 F)
2 tsp. canola oil (to
make omelet) (2 F)
Tomatoes and spinach (free)
2 slices low-fat cheese (2 P)

Lunch
Large salad (1 C)
2 Tbsp. light dressing (1 F)
3 ounces of fish, chicken,
lean meat (3 P)
½ cup chick peas (1 C) (1 P)

Snack
¾ cup Kashi's *Good
Friends* cereal (1 C)
6 pistachio nuts (1 F)

Dinner
Eggplant Parmigiana
Hero *recipe* (5 C)
1 slice low-fat cheese (1 P)

Snack
1 crepe, ½ banana and
¼ cup berries (1 C)
2 Tbsp. light whipped
cream (free)

Day Twenty-Eight

Breakfast
1 whole-wheat English
muffin (2 C)
2 slices Jarlsberg light
cheese (2 P)
1 poached egg (1 P) (1 F)
2 slices tomato

Lunch
Spinach Pie *recipe*
(2 P) (1 C) (1F)

Snack
1 light fruit yogurt (1 C) (1 P)
¾ cup Kashi's *Good
Friends* cereal (1 C)
2 walnuts (1 F)

Dinner
Shrimp, Vegetable, and
Pasta Casserole *recipe*
(2C) (3 P) (2 F)

Snack
6 almonds (1 F)
2 fruits (2 C)

*It's time for your weekly weigh-in. See how
much you've already accomplished!*

Day Twenty-Nine	Day Thirty
Breakfast	**Breakfast**
½ cup low-fat cottage cheese (2 P)	Fruit shake: blend 1 ripe banana with ¾ cup berries and 8 ounces low-fat milk (3 C) (1 P)
1 fruit (1 C)	
Lunch	**Lunch**
Large salad (1 C)	Large salad (1 C)
2 Tbsp. light dressing (1 F)	2 Tbsp. light dressing (1 F)
3 ounces shrimp (3 P)	3 ounces chicken, baked (3 P)
10 peanuts (1 F)	1 slice low-fat cheese (1 P)
Snack	1 hard-boiled egg (1 P) (1 F)
1 light fruit yogurt (1 C) (1 P)	**Snack**
6 pistachio nuts (1 F)	1 light fruit yogurt (1 C) (1 P)
Dinner	6 almonds (1 F)
Vegetable Chow Mein *recipe* (2 C) (1 F)	**Dinner**
Add 3 ounces of chicken or shrimp (3 P)	Veggie Mexican *recipe* (3 C) (2 P) (1 F)
Snack	**Snack**
2 Applesauce-Oatmeal Cookies *recipe* (4 C) (2 F)	12 cashews (2 F)
25-calorie fat-free hot cocoa (free)	1 fruit (1 C)
	Sugar-free Jell-O (free)

Request foods in restaurants with dressings on the side, light on the sauce and no added cheese to significantly reduce calories!

Dottie's 1600-Mile Journey
Sample Daily Tracker

1600 Miles	Carbohydrate: 11 servings	Protein: 10 servings	Fat: 6 servings

You are allowed the following amounts of carbohydrates, proteins and fats. Choose them wisely! Check off the boxes as you consume each serving.

C=Carbohydrates (starch, fruit, milk, vegetables): 1 serving has 15 grams of total carbohydrate. Pick 11 servings. Refer to food serving size list.

15 g	15 g	15 g	15 g	15 g	15 g
15 g	15 g	15 g	15 g	15 g	XXXX

P=Proteins (fish, poultry, meat, eggs, cheese, tofu, etc.): Choose mostly very lean or lean. 1 serving has 7 grams of protein or 1 ounce. Pick 10 servings.

7 g	7 g	7 g	7 g	7 g
7 g	7 g	7 g	7 g	7 g

F=Fats (oils, nuts, butters, etc.): Choose mostly monounsaturated fats. 1 serving has 5 grams of fat. Pick 6 servings.

5 g	5 g	5 g	5 g	5 g	5 g

W=Water

16 ounces	16 ounces	16 ounces	16 ounces

Dottie's 1600-Mile Weekly Tracker

DAY 1	C	C	C	C	C	C	C	C	C	C	C
	P	P	P	P	P	P	P	P	P	P	
	F	F	F	F	F	F					
DAY 2	C	C	C	C	C	C	C	C	C	C	C
	P	P	P	P	P	P	P	P	P	P	
	F	F	F	F	F	F					
DAY 3	C	C	C	C	C	C	C	C	C	C	C
	P	P	P	P	P	P	P	P	P	P	
	F	F	F	F	F	F					
DAY 4	C	C	C	C	C	C	C	C	C	C	C
	P	P	P	P	P	P	P	P	P	P	
	F	F	F	F	F	F					
DAY 5	C	C	C	C	C	C	C	C	C	C	C
	P	P	P	P	P	P	P	P	P	P	
	F	F	F	F	F	F					
DAY 6	C	C	C	C	C	C	C	C	C	C	C
	P	P	P	P	P	P	P	P	P	P	
	F	F	F	F	F	F					
DAY 7	C	C	C	C	C	C	C	C	C	C	C
	P	P	P	P	P	P	P	P	P	P	
	F	F	F	F	F	F					

Love yourself. These changes will lead you to real and complete happiness. Take it one day at a time. Take a deep breath and get ready to improve your health.

Dottie's 1600-Mile Weekly Tracker

DAY 1	C	C	C	C	C	C	C	C	C	C	C
	P	P	P	P	P	P	P	P	P	P	
	F	F	F	F	F	F					
DAY 2	C	C	C	C	C	C	C	C	C	C	C
	P	P	P	P	P	P	P	P	P	P	
	F	F	F	F	F	F					
DAY 3	C	C	C	C	C	C	C	C	C	C	C
	P	P	P	P	P	P	P	P	P	P	
	F	F	F	F	F	F					
DAY 4	C	C	C	C	C	C	C	C	C	C	C
	P	P	P	P	P	P	P	P	P	P	
	F	F	F	F	F	F					
DAY 5	C	C	C	C	C	C	C	C	C	C	C
	P	P	P	P	P	P	P	P	P	P	
	F	F	F	F	F	F					
DAY 6	C	C	C	C	C	C	C	C	C	C	C
	P	P	P	P	P	P	P	P	P	P	
	F	F	F	F	F	F					
DAY 7	C	C	C	C	C	C	C	C	C	C	C
	P	P	P	P	P	P	P	P	P	P	
	F	F	F	F	F	F					

Beans, vegetables and grains are very high
in fiber and will help to fill you up!

Dottie's 1600-Mile Weekly Tracker

DAY 1	C	C	C	C	C	C	C	C	C	C	C
	P	P	P	P	P	P	P	P	P	P	
	F	F	F	F	F	F					
DAY 2	C	C	C	C	C	C	C	C	C	C	C
	P	P	P	P	P	P	P	P	P	P	
	F	F	F	F	F	F					
DAY 3	C	C	C	C	C	C	C	C	C	C	C
	P	P	P	P	P	P	P	P	P	P	
	F	F	F	F	F	F					
DAY 4	C	C	C	C	C	C	C	C	C	C	C
	P	P	P	P	P	P	P	P	P	P	
	F	F	F	F	F	F					
DAY 5	C	C	C	C	C	C	C	C	C	C	C
	P	P	P	P	P	P	P	P	P	P	
	F	F	F	F	F	F					
DAY 6	C	C	C	C	C	C	C	C	C	C	C
	P	P	P	P	P	P	P	P	P	P	
	F	F	F	F	F	F					
DAY 7	C	C	C	C	C	C	C	C	C	C	C
	P	P	P	P	P	P	P	P	P	P	
	F	F	F	F	F	F					

Drink a glass of water, herbal tea or low-sodium V8 juice before you start your meal.

Dottie's 1600-Mile Weekly Tracker

DAY 1	C	C	C	C	C	C	C	C	C	C	C
	P	P	P	P	P	P	P	P	P	P	
	F	F	F	F	F	F					
DAY 2	C	C	C	C	C	C	C	C	C	C	C
	P	P	P	P	P	P	P	P	P	P	
	F	F	F	F	F	F					
DAY 3	C	C	C	C	C	C	C	C	C	C	C
	P	P	P	P	P	P	P	P	P	P	
	F	F	F	F	F	F					
DAY 4	C	C	C	C	C	C	C	C	C	C	C
	P	P	P	P	P	P	P	P	P	P	
	F	F	F	F	F	F					
DAY 5	C	C	C	C	C	C	C	C	C	C	C
	P	P	P	P	P	P	P	P	P	P	
	F	F	F	F	F	F					
DAY 6	C	C	C	C	C	C	C	C	C	C	C
	P	P	P	P	P	P	P	P	P	P	
	F	F	F	F	F	F					
DAY 7	C	C	C	C	C	C	C	C	C	C	C
	P	P	P	P	P	P	P	P	P	P	
	F	F	F	F	F	F					

Modifications.
Your decisions will improve your life!
You are worth it and deserve it!

Dottie's 1600-Mile 2-Week Shortcut

<u>*Day One*</u>	<u>*Day Two*</u>
Breakfast	**Breakfast**
1 whole-wheat English muffin (2 C)	1 cup cooked oatmeal made with water (2 C)
2 ounces goat cheese (2 P)	1 Fruit (1 C)
Lunch	2 walnuts, chopped (1 F)
Large salad (1 C)	1 slice whole-wheat bread (1 C)
3 ounces tuna (3 P)	**Lunch**
2 Tbsp. light dressing (1 F)	2 slices whole-wheat bread (2 C)
10 peanuts (1 F)	3 ounces turkey (3 P)
½ cup chickpeas (1 C) (1 P)	Mustard
6 whole-grain crackers (1 C)	Lettuce and tomato
Snack	**Snack**
1 fruit (1 C)	Baked apple (1 C)
12 almonds (2 F)	4 walnuts, chopped (2 F)
Dinner	**Dinner**
1 large bowl of Veggie Soup *recipe* (1 C)	Salad with 2 tsp. olive oil plus vinegar (2 F)
4 ounces shrimp, grilled with spices (4 P)	2 cups broccoli, steamed with 1 cup no-salt canned diced tomatoes (2 C)
2 cups vegetables steamed with 1 cup no-salt diced tomatoes (2 C)	6 ounces salmon (6 P)
Snack	**Snack**
12 almonds (2 F)	2 fruit (2 C)
2 fruits (2 C)	6 almonds, slivered (1 F)

Today is your first day. Make sure to weigh yourself so you will see your results!

Day Three
Breakfast
1 cup cooked *Wheatena* (2 C)
1 fruit (1 C)
2 walnuts, chopped (1 F)
Cinnamon
Snack
1 light fruit yogurt (1 C) (1 P)
6 almonds (1 F)
Lunch
Caesar Salad *recipe*
(1 C) (1 P) (2 F)
Add 3 ounces shrimp (3 P)
6 whole-wheat crackers (1 C)
Snack
12 ounces low-sodium V8 or
tomato juice (1 C)
Dinner
Large bowl of Veggie Soup
recipe (1 C)
5 ounces of chicken (5 P)
Large Salad (1 C)
2 Tbsp. light dressing (1 F)
Snack
2 fruits (2 C)
6 cashews (1 F)

Day Four
Breakfast
2 slices whole-grain bread (2 C)
½ cup fat-free or 1% cottage
cheese (2 P)
1 cup fresh fruit (1 C)
Lunch
2 slices rye bread (2 C)
3 ounces tuna (3 P)
1 Tbsp. light mayonnaise (1 F)
1 fruit (1 C)
Snack
3-4 cups of popcorn (1 C)
Dinner
Salad with 2 Tbsp. light
dressing (1 F)
10 low-sodium black olives (1 F)
5 ounces fish or poultry
(5 P) grilled with spices
3 cups broccoli (2 C)
1 tsp. olive oil drizzled on top of
vegetables (1 F)
Snack
2 fruits (2 C)
12 almonds (2 F)

Eat slowly! It takes 20 minutes for your brain to realize you've eaten! Eating quickly leads to overeating!

Day Five	*Day Six*
Breakfast	**Breakfast**
1 English muffin (2 C)	2 frozen *Go Lean* low-fat, whole-grain waffles (2 C)
1 egg fried in *Pam* spray (1 P) (1 F)	2 Tbsp. maple syrup (2 C)
1 slice low-fat cheese (1 P)	**Lunch**
1 fruit (1 C)	Large salad (1 C)
Snack	3 ounces chicken (3 P)
6 whole-grain crackers (1 C)	10 peanuts (1 F)
Lunch	1 Tbsp. olive oil plus vinegar (3 F)
2 slices whole-wheat bread (2 C)	6 whole-grain crackers (1 C)
2 ounces shrimp or chicken salad (2 P)	**Snack**
1 Tbsp. light mayonnaise (for salad) (1 F)	12 ounces low-sodium V8 juice (1 C)
Snack	**Dinner**
1 light fruit yogurt (1 C) (1 P)	3 cups vegetables steamed with 2 Tbsp. salsa (2 C)
6 almonds (1 F)	5 ounces shrimp, grilled or baked with spices (5 P)
Dinner	2 slices low-fat shredded cheese melted on top (2 P)
1 Tbsp. olive oil (3 F) to sauté 3 cups vegetables (2 C)	**Snack**
5 ounces fish, poultry, or lean meat (5 P)	¾ cup Kashi's *Good Friends* cereal (1 C)
Snack	3 dried apricots (1 C)
Sugar-free Jell-O (free)	12 cashews (2 F)
2 fruits (2 C)	

Never give up! You are strong and you will succeed at your goal. Take the highway to health... there are no shortcuts.

Day Seven

Breakfast

1 cup cooked oatmeal made with water (2 C)
1 small banana (1 C)
2 walnuts, chopped (1 F)

Snack

1 light fruit yogurt (1 C) (1 P)
¾ cup Kashi's *Good Friends* cereal (1 C)

Lunch

Avocado, Shrimp, Roasted Garlic and Walnut Salad *recipe* (1 C) (3 P) (3 F)

Snack

1 fruit (1 C)
6 almonds (1 F)

Dinner

6 ounces shrimp (6 P) sautéed with 1 Tbsp. olive oil (1 F)
3 cups non-starchy vegetables (2 C)

Snack

Sugar-free Jell-O (free)
2 fruits (2 C)

Day Eight

Breakfast

1 pumpernickel bagel (4 C)
2 slice low-fat cheese (2 P)
2 eggs, poached (2 P) (2 F)

Lunch

Large salad (1 C)
Vinaigrette Dressing *recipe* (2 F)
1 cup grilled tofu (2 P)
1 fruit (1 C)

Snack

12 ounces low-sodium V8 juice (1 C)

Dinner

4 ounces scallops, broiled (4 P)
2 ½ cups green vegetables and ½ cup diced tomatoes (2 C)

Snack

2 fruits (2 C)
20 peanuts (2 F)

It's time for your weekly weigh-in. See how much you've already accomplished!

<u>*Day Nine*</u>	<u>*Day Ten*</u>
Breakfast	**Breakfast**
1 ½ cups *Good Friends* (2 C)	1 fruit (1 C)
1 cup skim milk (1 C) (1 P)	1 cup cooked oatmeal made
1 fruit (1 C)	with water (2 C)
Snack	2 walnuts, chopped (1 F)
1 fruit (1 C)	**Lunch**
Lunch	2 slices rye bread (2 C)
2 slices whole-wheat bread	3 ounces tuna (3 P)
(2 C)	1 Tbsp. light mayonnaise (1 F)
1 cup grilled tofu (2 P)	1 fruit (1 C)
1/3 cup Hummus *recipe*	**Snack**
(1 C) (1 P)	1 low-fat yogurt 6 oz. (1 C) (1 P)
Broccoli sprouts	¾ cup Kashi's *Good Friends*
Snack	cereal (1 C)
1 light fruit yogurt (1 C) (1 P)	2 walnuts (1 F)
12 almonds (2 F)	**Dinner**
Dinner	*Dining out*:
Salad with 1 tsp. olive oil plus	Caesar salad with no croutons,
vinegar (1 F)	and dressing on the side
1 ½ cups green vegetables	(1 C) (3 F)
(1 C)	6 ounces grilled fish or poultry
5 ounces grilled fish (5 P)	(6 P)
Snack	**Snack**
30 peanuts (3 F)	2 fruits (2 C)
1 fruit (1 C)	Sugar-free Jell-O (free)

Calories sneak up on you! You can lose one pound each week by decreasing your calories by 500 each day. 12 ounces of orange juice is 200 calories and 2 tablespoons of olive oil is 240!

Day Eleven
Breakfast
1 ½ cups high-fiber cereal (5 grams of fiber or more) (2 C)
½ cup skim milk and ½ fruit serving (1 C)
4 walnuts, chopped (2 F)
Lunch
6 " *Subway* sandwich (3 C) no cheese
2 Tbsp. light dressing or 1 Tbsp. light mayonnaise (1 F)
2 ounces turkey, teriyaki chicken, seafood salad, tuna (already has mayonnaise) or garden burger (2 P)
Snack
12 ounces low-sodium V8 or tomato juice (1 C)
Dinner
6 ounces boneless pork tenderloin (6 P)
3 cups vegetables (2 C)
2 ounces low-fat shredded cheese (2 P)
Snack
18 cashews (3 F)
2 fruits (2 C)

Day Twelve
Breakfast
1 ½ cups *Wheatena* made with water (3 C)
1 fruit (1 C)
2 walnuts, chopped (1 F)
Cinnamon
Lunch
1 large slice pizza plain or with vegetables (2 C) (2 P) (2 F)
Snack
1 fruit (1 C)
¼ cup cottage cheese (1 P)
Dinner
6 ounces fish, poultry, or lean meat (6 P)
3 cups vegetables (2 C)
1 slice low-fat cheese melted on top (1 P)
2 Tbsp. avocado (1 F)
Snack
2 fruits (2 C)
12 almonds (2 F)

Out with the old poor eating habits and in with the new and improved eating habits.

Day Thirteen	*Day Fourteen*
Breakfast	**Breakfast**
1 ½ cups high-fiber cereal (2 C)	1 large pumpernickel bagel (4 C)
1 cup low-fat milk (1 C) (1 P)	1 poached egg (1 P) (1 F)
1 fruit serving (1 C)	1 slice low-fat cheese (1 P)
Lunch	1 Tbsp. light whipped butter (1 F)
Large salad (1 C)	1 slice tomato
3 ounces tuna (3 P)	**Lunch**
2 Tbsp. light dressing (1 F)	Large salad (1 C)
½ cup chickpeas (1 C) (1 P)	3 ounces baked salmon (3 P)
Snack	½ cup chick peas (1 C) (1 P)
1 fruit (1 C)	2 Tbsp. light dressing (1 F)
6 almonds (1 F)	**Snack**
Dinner	1 fruit (1 C)
5 ounces chicken (5 P)	6 almonds (1 F)
sautéed with 2 tsp. olive oil (2 F)	**Dinner**
3 cups non-starchy vegetables (2 C)	4 ounces fish, grilled (4 P)
Snack	3 cups non-starchy vegetables (2 C),
2 fruits (2 C)	sautéed with 2 tsp. olive oil (2 F)
12 cashews (2 F)	**Snack**
25-calorie fat-free hot cocoa (free)	Sugar-free Jell-O (free)
	2 fruits (2 C)

It's time for your weekly weigh-in. See how much you've already accomplished!

Have you lost weight during these first two weeks? If not, review the rules and start from Day One! You can do it!

Be sure to drink your water daily!

DOTTIE

Regular eating patterns – for life!

Day Fifteen	Day Sixteen
Breakfast	**Breakfast**
2 slices whole-grain bread (2 C)	High-Fiber Muffin *recipe*
¾ cup low-fat cottage cheese (3 P) with cinnamon melted on top	(1 C) (1 F)
Lunch	**Lunch**
2 slices pumpernickel bread (2 C)	Marinated Bean and Vegetable Salad *recipe* (1 C) (1 P) (2 F)
3 ounces turkey (3 P)	**Snack**
1 slice low-fat cheese (1 P)	12 ounces low-sodium V8 juice (1 C)
Lettuce and tomato	6 whole-grain crackers (1 C)
Snack	1 slice low-fat cheese (1 P)
6 crackers (1 C)	**Dinner**
Eggplant Caponata á la Lois *recipe* (3 F) (1 C)	6 ounces flounder, baked (6 P)
Dinner	1 Tbsp. olive oil to stir fry (3 F):
Scallops and Broccoli *recipe* (3 P) (1 C) (1 F)	1 cup black beans (2 C) (2 P)
2/3 cup cooked whole-wheat pasta (2 C)	3 cups non-starchy vegetables (2 C)
Snack	**Snack**
Sugar-free Jell-O (free)	2 fruits (2 C)
2 fruits (2 C)	3-4 cups popcorn (1 C)
25-calorie fat-free hot cocoa (free)	
20 peanuts (2 F)	

Look around at the people who have the body you want. They work hard for it! They make wise food choices most of the time and probably exercise regularly.

### *Day Seventeen*	### *Day Eighteen*
Breakfast	**Breakfast**
1 cup cooked oatmeal made with water (2 C)	1 ½ cups high-fiber cereal (2 C)
4 walnuts (2 F)	½ cup low fat milk and ½ fruit serving (1 C)
2 Tbsp. flaxseed meal, unprocessed oat bran, or unprocessed bran (1 C)	**Lunch**
1 fruit (1 C)	Large salad (1 C)
Snack	2 Tbsp. light dressing (1 F)
1 light fruit yogurt (1 C) (1 P)	10 low-sodium black olives (1 F)
Lunch	3 ounces baked chicken (3 P)
2 slices whole-grain bread (2 C)	1 hard-boiled egg (1 P) (1 F)
3 ounces tuna (3 P)	**Snack**
1 Tbsp. light mayonnaise (1 F)	15 baked tortilla chips (1 C)
1 fruit (1 C)	1 serving Black Bean and Corn Dip *recipe* (2 C) (1 P)
Snack	**Dinner**
12 ounces of low-sodium V8 juice (1 C)	5 ounces grilled salmon (5 P)
Dinner	1 cup cooked kasha (2 C)
Poached salmon *recipe* (6 P)	1 ½ cups green vegetables (1 C)
Brussels sprouts *recipe* (2 F) (½ C)	**Snack**
Snack	18 cashews (3 F)
1 large baked apple made with cinnamon (1 ½ C)	1 fruit (1 C)
2 walnuts (1 F)	

DO NOT PUNISH YOURSELF just because you want to lose weight and be healthy! Make reasonable choices that you can live with for the rest of your life!

Day Nineteen	Day Twenty
Breakfast	**Breakfast**
High-fiber muffin *recipe* (1 C) (1 F)	Oat bran Flaxseed Muffin *recipe* (2 C) (1 F)
4 ounces fruit juice (1 C)	4 ounces fruit juice (1 C)
Snack	**Lunch**
6 whole-grain crackers (1 C)	2 slices whole-wheat pita bread (2 C)
1 slice low-fat cheese (1 P)	3 ounces turkey (3 P)
Lunch	1 Tbsp. light mayonnaise (1 F)
2 slices bread (2 C)	2 Tbsp. avocado (1 F)
3 ounces turkey (3 P)	Lettuce, tomatoes, sprouts
1 slice low-fat cheese (1 P)	1 fruit (1 C)
Lettuce and tomato	**Snack**
1 fruit (1 C)	Hummus *recipe* (1 C) (1 P)
Snack	1 cup vegetables to dip
Eggplant Dip *recipe* (1 C) (1 F)	**Dinner**
6 crackers and 1 cup vegetables (1 C)	Fried Flounder *recipe* (6 P) (1 C)
Dinner	Cauliflower Casserole *recipe* (1C)(1 F)
Shrimp, Tomato, Spinach and Feta *recipe* (4 P) (1 F) (1 C)	**Snack**
Bulgur Pilaf *recipe* (1 C) (1 F)	2 fruits (2 C)
Snack	12 almonds (2 F)
1 light fruit yogurt 6 oz. (1 C) (1 P)	
12 cashews (2 F)	

Play for Life!
Put yourself first. Take control of your
life. You will never regret it.

Day Twenty-One	*Day Twenty-Two*
Breakfast	**Breakfast**
1 cup cooked oatmeal made with water (2 C)	2 slices toast (2 C)
4 walnuts, chopped (2 F)	½ cup low-fat cottage cheese (2 P)
1 fruit (1 C)	**Snack**
Cinnamon	1 light fruit yogurt (1 C) (1 P)
Lunch	6 almonds (1 F)
Large salad (1 C)	**Lunch**
½ cup chickpeas (1 C) (1 P)	Large salad (1 C)
3 ounces shrimp (3 P)	2 tsp. olive oil plus vinegar (2 F)
10 low-sodium olives (1 F)	2 ounces goat cheese (2 P)
2 Tbsp. light dressing (1 F)	3 ounces fish (3 P)
6 whole-grain crackers (1 C)	**Snack**
Snack	Fruit Shake *¾ cup berries, 4 ounces skim milk, ½ ripe banana and ice* (2 C)
Low-fat spinach dip *recipe* (1 C)	**Dinner**
1 cup vegetables to dip	1 hamburger bun (2 C)
Dinner	1 Vegetable Burger (2 P)
Salmon Teriyaki, Kasha and Vegetables *recipe* (6 P) (3 C)	6-ounce medium potato (baked as fries) *recipe* (2 C)
Snack	Homemade coleslaw *recipe* (1F)
Sugar-free Jell-O (free)	**Snack**
1 fruit (1 C)	1 fruit (1 C)
12 cashews (2 F)	12 almonds (2 F)

It's time for your weekly weigh-in. See how much you've already accomplished!

Day Twenty-Three	Day Twenty-Four
Breakfast	**Breakfast**
High-fiber muffin *recipe* (1 C) (1 F)	1 whole-wheat bagel (4 C)
4 ounces fruit juice (1 C)	1 poached egg (1 P) (1 F)
	1 slice low-fat cheese (1 P)
Lunch	**Lunch**
2 slices whole-grain bread (2 C)	Portabella Mushroom Sandwich
3 ounces turkey (3 P)	*recipe* (1 C) (2 P)
Lettuce and tomato	1 fruit (1 C)
Snack	**Snack**
8 animal crackers (1 C)	6 vanilla wafers (1 C)
25-calorie fat-free hot cocoa (free)	25-calorie fat-free hot cocoa (free)
Dinner	**Dinner**
6 ounces grilled fish (6 P)	4 ounces grilled salmon (4 P)
2 tsp. olive oil (2 F)	Potato-Zucchini Cake *recipe*
1 cup cooked kasha (2 C)	(1 P) (2 C) (2 F)
3 cups cooked broccoli (2 C)	**Snack**
Snack	1 cup low-fat ice cream
1 cup low-fat ice cream (2 C) (1 F) (1 P)	(2 C) (1 F) (1 P)
4 walnuts (2 F)	4 walnuts (2 F)

Having trouble modifying your eating habits? Think of why you failed at diets and why you can succeed by slowly changing your behavior toward food. Give yourself a chance!

Day Twenty-Five
Breakfast
1 ½ cups Kashi's *Good Friends* cereal (2 C)
1 cup skim milk (1 C) (1 P)
1 fruit (1 C)
Lunch
Garden burger (2 P)
1 slice low-fat cheese (1 P)
1 hamburger bun (2 C)
Broccoli sprouts
2 Tbsp. avocado (1 F)
Snack
1 fruit (1 C)
12 cashews (2 F)
Dinner
6 ounces grilled chicken (6 P)
1 medium 6-oz. sweet potato (baked as chips) *recipe* (2 C)
1 ½ cups cooked vegetables, steamed (1 C)
Snack
1 fruit (1 C)
6 almonds and 4 walnuts (3 F)

Day Twenty-Six
Breakfast
2 slices whole-wheat bread (2 C)
½ cup cottage cheese (2 P)
Lunch
2 slices whole-wheat bread (2 C)
2 ounces tuna (2 P)
1 Tbsp. light mayonnaise (1 F)
Snack
6 – 8 cups popcorn (2 C)
Dinner
5 ounces fish, poultry, or lean meat, baked (5 P)
Tabouleh *recipe* (1 C) (1 F)
3 cups steamed broccoli (2 C)
6 almonds slivered on broccoli (1 F)
Snack
1 cup low-fat ice cream (2 C) (1 F) (1 P)
4 walnuts (2 F)

Question.
Every food or beverage you consume should be considered.

Day Twenty-Seven	*Day Twenty-Eight*
Breakfast	**Breakfast**
2-egg omelet (2 P) (2 F)	1 whole-wheat bagel (4 C)
2 tsp. canola oil (to make omelet) (2 F)	2 slices Jarlsberg light cheese (2 P)
Tomatoes and spinach (free)	2 poached eggs (2 P) (2 F)
2 slices low-fat cheese (2 P)	2 slices tomato
½ large pumpernickel bagel (2 C)	**Lunch**
1 Tbsp. light whipped butter (1 F)	Spinach Pie *recipe* (2 P) (1 C) (1F)
Lunch	**Snack**
Large salad (1 C)	1 light fruit yogurt (1 C) (1 P)
2 Tbsp. light dressing (1 F)	¾ cup Kashi's *Good Friends* cereal (1 C)
3 ounces fish (3 P)	**Dinner**
½ cup chickpeas (1 C) (1 P)	Shrimp, Vegetable, and Pasta Casserole *recipe*
Snack	(2C) (3 P) (2 F)
¾ cup Kashi's *Good Friends* cereal (1 C)	**Snack**
Dinner	6 almonds (1 F)
Eggplant Parmigiana Hero (5 C)	2 fruits (2 C)
2 slices low-fat cheese (2 P)	
Snack	
1 crepe, ½ banana and ¼ cup berries (1 C)	
2 Tbsp. light whipped cream (free)	

It's time for your weekly weigh-in. See how much you've already accomplished!

Day Twenty-Nine	*Day Thirty*
Breakfast	**Breakfast**
½ cup low-fat cottage cheese (2 P)	Fruit shake: blend 1 ripe banana with ¾ cup berries and 8 ounces low-fat milk (3 C) (1 P)
1 whole-wheat English muffin (2 C)	2 poached eggs (2 P) (2 F)
1 fruit (1 C)	**Lunch**
Lunch	Large salad (1 C)
Large salad (1 C)	2 Tbsp. light dressing (1 F)
2 Tbsp. light dressing (1 F)	3 ounces chicken, baked (3 P)
3 ounces shrimp (3 P)	1 slice low-fat cheese (1 P)
1 ounce goat cheese (1 P)	6 whole-grain crackers (1 C)
10 peanuts (1 F)	**Snack**
Snack	1 light fruit yogurt (1 C) (1 P)
1 light fruit yogurt (1 C) (1 P)	6 almonds (1 F)
6 pistachio nuts (1 F)	**Dinner**
Dinner	Veggie Mexican *recipe* (3 C) (2 P) (1 F)
Vegetable Chow Mein *recipe* (2 C) (1 F)	**Snack**
Add 3 ounces chicken or shrimp (3 P)	6 cashews (1 F)
Snack	2 fruits (2 C)
2 Applesauce-Oatmeal Cookies *recipe* (4 C) (2 F)	Sugar-free Jell-O (free)
25-calorie fat-free hot cocoa (free)	

Are you recording food choices, exercise and feelings in your journal?

Randy's 1800-Mile Journey

Sample Daily Tracker

1800 Miles	Carbohydrate: 12 servings	Protein: 11 servings	Fat: 7 servings

You are allowed the following amounts of carbohydrates, proteins and fats. Choose them wisely! Check off the boxes as you consume each serving.

C=Carbohydrates (starch, fruit, milk, vegetables): 1 serving has 15 grams of total carbohydrate. Pick 12 servings. Refer to food serving size list.

15 g	15 g	15 g	15 g	15 g	15 g
15 g	15 g	15 g	15 g	15 g	15 g

P=Proteins (fish, poultry, meat, eggs, cheese, tofu, etc.): Choose mostly very lean or lean. 1 serving has 7 grams of protein or 1 ounce. Pick 11 servings.

7 g	7 g	7 g	7 g	7 g	7 g
7 g	7 g	7 g	7 g	7 g	XXXX

F=Fats (oils, nuts, butters, etc.): Choose mostly monounsaturated fats. 1 serving has 5 grams of fat. Pick 7 servings.

5 g	5 g	5 g	5 g	5 g	5 g	5 g

W=Water

16 ounces	16 ounces	16 ounces	16 ounces

Randy's 1800-Mile Weekly Tracker

DAY 1	C	C	C	C	C	C	C	C	C	C	C	C
	P	P	P	P	P	P	P	P	P	P	P	
	F	F	F	F	F	F	F					
DAY 2	C	C	C	C	C	C	C	C	C	C	C	C
	P	P	P	P	P	P	P	P	P	P	P	
	F	F	F	F	F	F	F					
DAY 3	C	C	C	C	C	C	C	C	C	C	C	C
	P	P	P	P	P	P	P	P	P	P	P	
	F	F	F	F	F	F	F					
DAY 4	C	C	C	C	C	C	C	C	C	C	C	C
	P	P	P	P	P	P	P	P	P	P	P	
	F	F	F	F	F	F	F					
DAY 5	C	C	C	C	C	C	C	C	C	C	C	C
	P	P	P	P	P	P	P	P	P	P	P	
	F	F	F	F	F	F	F					
DAY 6	C	C	C	C	C	C	C	C	C	C	C	C
	P	P	P	P	P	P	P	P	P	P	P	
	F	F	F	F	F	F	F					
DAY 7	C	C	C	C	C	C	C	C	C	C	C	C
	P	P	P	P	P	P	P	P	P	P	P	
	F	F	F	F	F	F	F					

Rules.
We abide by traffic rules or there will be consequences. Let's abide by healthy eating rules to avoid those consequences as well.

Randy's 1800-Mile Weekly Tracker

DAY 1	C	C	C	C	C	C	C	C	C	C	C	C
	P	P	P	P	P	P	P	P	P	P	P	
	F	F	F	F	F	F	F					
DAY 2	C	C	C	C	C	C	C	C	C	C	C	C
	P	P	P	P	P	P	P	P	P	P	P	
	F	F	F	F	F	F	F					
DAY 3	C	C	C	C	C	C	C	C	C	C	C	C
	P	P	P	P	P	P	P	P	P	P	P	
	F	F	F	F	F	F	F					
DAY 4	C	C	C	C	C	C	C	C	C	C	C	C
	P	P	P	P	P	P	P	P	P	P	P	
	F	F	F	F	F	F	F					
DAY 5	C	C	C	C	C	C	C	C	C	C	C	C
	P	P	P	P	P	P	P	P	P	P	P	
	F	F	F	F	F	F	F					
DAY 6	C	C	C	C	C	C	C	C	C	C	C	C
	P	P	P	P	P	P	P	P	P	P	P	
	F	F	F	F	F	F	F					
DAY 7	C	C	C	C	C	C	C	C	C	C	C	C
	P	P	P	P	P	P	P	P	P	P	P	
	F	F	F	F	F	F	F					

Have you had at least 8 eight-ounce glasses of water or herbal tea today?

Randy's 1800-Mile Weekly Tracker

DAY 1	C	C	C	C	C	C	C	C	C	C	C	C
	P	P	P	P	P	P	P	P	P	P	P	
	F	F	F	F	F	F	F					
DAY 2	C	C	C	C	C	C	C	C	C	C	C	C
	P	P	P	P	P	P	P	P	P	P	P	
	F	F	F	F	F	F	F					
DAY 3	C	C	C	C	C	C	C	C	C	C	C	C
	P	P	P	P	P	P	P	P	P	P	P	
	F	F	F	F	F	F	F					
DAY 4	C	C	C	C	C	C	C	C	C	C	C	C
	P	P	P	P	P	P	P	P	P	P	P	
	F	F	F	F	F	F	F					
DAY 5	C	C	C	C	C	C	C	C	C	C	C	C
	P	P	P	P	P	P	P	P	P	P	P	
	F	F	F	F	F	F	F					
DAY 6	C	C	C	C	C	C	C	C	C	C	C	C
	P	P	P	P	P	P	P	P	P	P	P	
	F	F	F	F	F	F	F					
DAY 7	C	C	C	C	C	C	C	C	C	C	C	C
	P	P	P	P	P	P	P	P	P	P	P	
	F	F	F	F	F	F	F					

Consume food or a nutrient-rich beverage every
3-4 hours to sustain your metabolism.

Randy's 1800-Mile Weekly Tracker

DAY 1	C	C	C	C	C	C	C	C	C	C	C	C
	P	P	P	P	P	P	P	P	P	P	P	
	F	F	F	F	F	F	F					
DAY 2	C	C	C	C	C	C	C	C	C	C	C	C
	P	P	P	P	P	P	P	P	P	P	P	
	F	F	F	F	F	F	F					
DAY 3	C	C	C	C	C	C	C	C	C	C	C	C
	P	P	P	P	P	P	P	P	P	P	P	
	F	F	F	F	F	F	F					
DAY 4	C	C	C	C	C	C	C	C	C	C	C	C
	P	P	P	P	P	P	P	P	P	P	P	
	F	F	F	F	F	F	F					
DAY 5	C	C	C	C	C	C	C	C	C	C	C	C
	P	P	P	P	P	P	P	P	P	P	P	
	F	F	F	F	F	F	F					
DAY 6	C	C	C	C	C	C	C	C	C	C	C	C
	P	P	P	P	P	P	P	P	P	P	P	
	F	F	F	F	F	F	F					
DAY 7	C	C	C	C	C	C	C	C	C	C	C	C
	P	P	P	P	P	P	P	P	P	P	P	
	F	F	F	F	F	F	F					

Self-esteem.
Overeating hinders it. Being a
conscientious consumer aids in it!

Randy's 1800-Mile 2-Week Shortcut

Day One	*Day Two*
Breakfast	**Breakfast**
1 whole-wheat English muffin (2 C)	1 cup cooked oatmeal (2 C)
1 ounce goat cheese (1 P)	1 fruit (1 C)
1 light fruit yogurt (1 C) (1 P)	2 walnuts, chopped (1 F)
6 almonds (1 F)	1 slice whole-wheat bread (1 C)
Lunch	1 slice low-fat cheese (1 P)
3 cups salad (1 C)	**Snack**
3 ounces tuna (3 P)	1 light fruit yogurt (1 C) (1 P)
2 Tbsp. light dressing (1 F)	6 almonds (1 F)
10 peanuts (1 F)	**Lunch**
6 whole-grain crackers (1 C)	2 slices whole-wheat bread (2 C)
Snack	3 ounces turkey (3 P)
1 fruit (1 C)	**Snack**
12 almonds (2 F)	Baked apple (1 C)
12 ounces low-sodium V8 juice (1 C)	4 walnuts, chopped (2 F)
Dinner	**Dinner**
1 large bowl of Veggie Soup *recipe* (1 C)	Salad with 2 tsp. olive oil plus vinegar (2 F)
6 ounces salmon, grilled with spices (6 P)	2 cups broccoli, steamed with 1 cup no-salt canned diced tomatoes (2 C)
2 cups vegetables, steamed with 1 cup no-salt diced tomatoes (2 C)	6 ounces salmon (6 P)
Snack	**Snack**
12 almonds (2 F)	2 fruit (2 C)
2 fruits (2 C)	6 almonds, slivered (1 F)

Today is your first day! Make sure to weigh yourself so you will see your results!

Day Three	**_Day Four_**
Breakfast	**Breakfast**
1 cup cooked *Wheatena* (2 C)	2 slices whole-grain bread (2 C)
1 fruit (1 C)	½ cup fat-free or 1% cottage
2 walnuts, chopped (1 F)	cheese (2 P)
Cinnamon	1 cup fresh fruit (1 C)
Snack	**Snack**
1 fruit (1 C)	1 light fruit yogurt (1 C) (1 P)
6 almonds (1 F)	6 almonds (1 F)
Lunch	**Lunch**
Caesar salad *recipe*	2 slices rye bread (2 C)
(1 C) (1 P) (2 F)	2 slices low-fat cheese (2 P)
Add 4 ounces shrimp (4 P)	2 slices tomato
6 whole-wheat crackers (1 C)	1 fruit (1 C)
Snack	**Snack**
1 fruit (1 C)	3-4 cups of popcorn (1 C)
6 almonds (1 F)	**Dinner**
Dinner	Salad with 2 Tbsp. light
6 ounces chicken (6 P)	dressing (1 F)
3 cups non-starchy vegetables	10 low-sodium black olives (1 F)
(2 C)	6 ounces fish (6 P)
1 tsp. oil (1 F)	3 cups broccoli (2 C)
Snack	1 tsp. olive oil drizzled on top of
2 fruits (2 C)	vegetables (1 F)
6 cashews (1 F)	6 almonds (1 F)
	Snack
	2 fruits (2 C)
	12 almonds (2 F)

Always use lettuce and tomatoes to bulk up your sandwich. Think vegetables, vegetables and more vegetables!

Day Five

Breakfast
1 English muffin (2 C)
1 egg fried in *Pam* spray
(1 P) (1 F)
1 slice low-fat cheese (1 P)
1 fruit (1 C)

Snack
¾ cup Kashi's *Good Friends* cereal (1 C)
3 dried apricots (1 C)
2 walnuts (1 F)

Lunch
2 slices whole-wheat bread (2C)
3 ounces shrimp or chicken salad (3 P)
1 Tbsp. light mayonnaise (for salad) (1 F)

Snack
1 light fruit yogurt (1 C) (1 P)
6 almonds (1 F)

Dinner
1 Tbsp. olive oil (3 F) to sauté 3 cups vegetables (2 C)
5 ounces fish, poultry, or lean meat (5 P)

Snack
2 fruits (2 C)

Day Six

Breakfast
2 frozen *Go Lean* low-fat, whole-grain waffles (2 C)
2 Tbsp. maple syrup (2 C)
1 fruit (1 C)

Lunch
Large salad (1 C)
3 ounces chicken (3 P)
10 peanuts (1 F)
1 Tbsp. olive oil plus vinegar (3 F)
6 whole-grain crackers (1 C)

Snack
1 fruit (1 C)
6 cashews (1 F)

Dinner
3 cups vegetables, steamed, with 2 Tbsp. salsa (2 C)
6 ounces shrimp, grilled or baked with spices (6 P)
2 slices low-fat shredded cheese melted on top (2 P)

Snack
¾ cup Kashi's *Good Friends* cereal (1 C)
3 dried apricots (1 C)
12 cashews (2 F)

Try.
Do your best to succeed. This achievement will bring you a lifetime of true happiness!

Day Seven	**_Day Eight_**
Breakfast	**Breakfast**
1 cup cooked oatmeal made with water (2 C)	1 pumpernickel bagel (4 C)
1 small banana (1 C)	2 slices low-fat cheese (2 P)
2 walnuts, chopped (1 F)	2 eggs, poached (2 P) (2 F)
1 slice whole-grain bread (1 C)	**Lunch**
¼ cup cottage cheese (1 P)	Large salad (1 C)
Snack	Vinaigrette Dressing *recipe* (2 F)
1 light fruit yogurt (1 C) (1 P)	3 ounces turkey (3 P)
¾ cup Kashi's *Good Friends* cereal (1 C)	1 fruit (1 C)
2 walnuts (1 F)	6 whole-wheat crackers (1 C)
Lunch	**Snack**
Avocado, Shrimp, Roasted Garlic and Walnut Salad *recipe* (1 C) (3 P) (3 F)	12 ounces low-sodium V8 juice (1 C)
Snack	**Dinner**
1 fruit (1 C)	4 ounces scallops, broiled (4 P)
6 almonds (1 F)	2 ½ cups green vegetables and ½ cup diced tomatoes (2 C)
Dinner	**Snack**
6 ounces shrimp (6 P) sautéed with 1 Tbsp. olive oil (1 F)	2 fruits (2 C)
3 cups non-starchy vegetables (2 C)	30 peanuts (3 F)
Snack	
Sugar-free Jell-O (free)	
2 fruits (2 C)	

It's time for your weekly weigh-in. See how much you've already accomplished!

Day Nine

Breakfast
1 ½ cups *Good Friends* (2 C)
1 cup skim milk (1 C) (1 P)
1 fruit (1 C)
1 slice whole-grain bread (1 C)
¼ cup cottage cheese (1 P)

Snack
1 fruit (1 C)
6 almonds (1 F)

Lunch
2 slices whole-wheat bread (2C)
1 cup grilled tofu (2 P)
1/3 cup Hummus *recipe*
(1 C) (1 P)
Broccoli sprouts

Snack
1 fruit (1 C)
12 almonds (2 F)

Dinner
Salad with 1 tsp. olive oil plus
vinegar (1 F)
1 ½ cups vegetables (1 C)
6 ounces grilled fish (6 P)

Snack
30 peanuts (3 F)
1 fruit (1 C)

Day Ten

Breakfast
1 fruit (1 C)
1 cup cooked oatmeal made
with water (2 C)
2 walnuts, chopped (1 F)

Snack
6 whole-wheat crackers (1 C)
1 slice low-fat cheese (1 P)

Lunch
2 slices rye bread (2 C)
3 ounces tuna (3 P)
1 Tbsp. light mayonnaise (1 F)
1 fruit (1 C)

Snack
1 light fruit yogurt (1 C) (1 P)
¾ cup Kashi's *Good Friends*
cereal (1 C)
4 walnuts (2 F)

Dinner
Dining out:
Caesar salad with no croutons,
and dressing on the side
(1 C) (1 P) (2 F)
5 ounces fish (5 P)

Snack
2 fruits (2 C)
6 almonds (1 F)

Unlock your power.
Use foods like healthy fats and fiber to
your advantage since they help to sustain
your appetite! Do not abuse them!

Day Eleven	*Day Twelve*
Breakfast	**Breakfast**
1 ½ cups cereal (5 grams of fiber or more) (2 C)	1 ½ cups *Wheatena* made with water (3 C)
½ cup skim milk and ½ fruit serving (1 C)	1 fruit (1 C)
4 walnuts, chopped (2 F)	4 walnuts, chopped (2 F)
	Cinnamon
Snack	**Snack**
¾ cup *Good Friends* (1 C)	1 fruit (1 C)
6 almonds (1 F)	6 almonds (1 F)
Lunch	**Lunch**
6 " *Subway* sandwich (3 C) no cheese	1 large slice pizza plain or with vegetables (2 C) (2 P) (2 F)
2 Tbsp. light dressing or 1 Tbsp. light mayonnaise (1 F)	**Snack**
3 ounces turkey, teriyaki chicken, seafood salad, tuna (already has mayonnaise) or garden burger (3 P)	1 fruit (1 C)
	½ cup cottage cheese (2 P)
Snack	**Dinner**
3-4 cups popcorn (1 C)	6 ounces fish, poultry, or lean meat (6 P)
Dinner	3 cups vegetables (2 C)
6 ounces poultry (6 P)	1 slice low-fat cheese melted on top (1 P)
3 cups vegetables (2 C)	**Snack**
2 ounces low-fat shredded cheese (2 P)	2 fruits (2 C)
Snack	12 almonds (2 F)
18 cashews (3 F)	
2 fruits (2 C)	

Being healthy saves you countless dollars on medications and medical bills. Use this extra money to reward yourself! Go to the spa or take a needed vacation!

Day Thirteen **Breakfast** 1 ½ cups high-fiber cereal (2 C) 1 cup low-fat milk (1 C) (1 P) 1 fruit serving (1 C) **Snack** ¾ cup *Good Friends* (1 C) 6 almonds (1 F) **Lunch** Large salad (1 C) 3 ounces tuna (3 P) 2 Tbsp. light dressing (1 F) ½ cup chickpeas (1 C) (1 P) **Snack** 1 fruit (1 C) 6 almonds (1 F) **Dinner** 6 ounces chicken (6 P), sautéed with 2 tsp. olive oil (2 F) 3 cups non-starchy vegetables (2 C) **Snack** 2 fruits (2 C) 12 cashews (2 F) 25-calorie fat-free hot cocoa (free)	**_Day Fourteen_** **Breakfast** 1 large pumpernickel bagel (4 C) 1 poached egg (1 P) (1 F) 1 slice low-fat cheese (1 P) 1 slice tomato **Lunch** Large salad (1 C) 3 ounces baked salmon (3 P) ½ cup chickpeas (1 C) (1 P) 2 Tbsp. light dressing (1 F) 6 whole-grain crackers (1 C) **Snack** 1 fruit (1 C) 6 almonds (1 F) **Dinner** 5 ounces fish, grilled (5 P) 3 cups non-starchy vegetables (2 C), sautéed with 1 Tbsp. olive oil (3 F) **Snack** Sugar-free Jell-O (free) 2 fruits (2 C) 6 cashews (1 F)

It's time for your weekly weigh-in. See how much you've already accomplished!

Have you lost weight during these first two weeks? If not, review the rules and start from Day One! You can do it!

Be sure to drink your water daily!

RANDY

Regular eating patterns – for life!

Day Fifteen	*Day Sixteen*
Breakfast	**Breakfast**
2 slices whole-grain bread (2 C)	High-Fiber Muffin *recipe*
¾ cup low-fat cottage cheese	(1 C) (1 F)
(3 P)	**Snack**
Snack	1 light fruit yogurt (1 C) (1 P)
1 light fruit yogurt (1 C) (1 P)	6 almonds (1 F)
6 almonds (1 F)	**Lunch**
Lunch	Marinated Bean and Vegetable
2 slices pumpernickel bread	Salad *recipe* (1 C) (1 P) (2 F)
(2 C)	**Snack**
3 ounces turkey (3 P)	12 ounces of low-sodium V8
1 slice low-fat cheese (1 P)	juice (1 C)
Lettuce and tomato	6 whole-grain crackers (1 C)
Snack	1 slice low-fat cheese (1 P)
6 crackers (1 C)	**Dinner**
Eggplant Caponata á la Lois	6 ounces flounder, baked (6 P)
recipe (3 F) (1 C)	1 Tbsp. olive oil to stir fry (3 F)
Dinner	1 cup black beans (2 C) (2 P)
Scallops and Broccoli *recipe*	3 cups non-starchy vegetables
(3 P) (1 C)(1 F)	(2 C)
2/3 cup cooked whole-wheat	**Snack**
pasta (2 C)	2 fruits (2 C)
Snack	3-4 cups popcorn (1 C)
Sugar-free Jell-O (free)	
2 fruits (2 C)	
25 calorie fat-free hot cocoa	
(free)	
20 peanuts (2 F)	

Victor not victim. Don't succumb to food's temptation. Win the battle. Be healthy and happy!

Day Seventeen	Day Eighteen
Breakfast	**Breakfast**
1 cup cooked oatmeal made with water (2 C)	1 ½ cups high-fiber cereal (2 C)
4 walnuts (2 F)	1 cup low-fat milk (1 C) (1 P)
2 Tbsp. flaxseed meal (1 C)	1 fruit serving (1 C)
¼ cup low-fat cottage cheese (1 P)	2 walnuts (1 F)
1 fruit (1 C)	**Lunch**
Snack	Large salad (1 C)
1 fruit (1 C)	2 Tbsp. light dressing (1 F)
6 almonds (1 F)	10 low sodium black olives (1 F)
Lunch	3 ounces baked chicken (3 P)
1 whole-grain pita (2 C)	1 hard-boiled egg (1 P) (1 F)
3 ounces tuna (3 P)	**Snack**
1 Tbsp. light mayonnaise (1 F)	15 baked tortilla chips (1 C)
1 fruit (1 C)	1 serving Black Bean and Corn Dip *recipe* (2 C) (1 P)
Snack	**Dinner**
6 crackers (1 C)	5 ounces grilled salmon (5 P)
Hummus *recipe* (1 C) (1 P)	1 cup cooked kasha (2 C)
Dinner	1 ½ cups green vegetables (1 C)
Poached salmon *recipe* (6 P)	**Snack**
Brussels sprouts *recipe* (2 F) (½ C)	18 cashews (3 F)
Snack	1 fruit (1 C)
1 large baked apple with cinnamon (1½ C)	
2 walnuts (1 F)	

We must be positive!

Day Nineteen
Breakfast
High-fiber muffin *recipe* (1 C) (1 F)
4 ounces fruit juice (1 C)
1 poached egg (1 P) (1 F)
Snack
6 whole-grain crackers (1 C)
1 slice low-fat cheese (1 P)
Lunch
2 slices bread (2 C)
3 ounces turkey (3 P)
1 slice low-fat cheese (1 P)
Lettuce and tomato
1 fruit (1 C)
Snack
Eggplant Dip *recipe* (1 C) (1 F)
12 crackers (2 C)
Dinner
Shrimp, Tomato, Spinach and Feta *recipe* (4 P) (1 F) (1 C)
Bulgur Pilaf *recipe* (1 C) (1 F)
Snack
1 light fruit yogurt 6 oz. (1 C) (1 P)
12 cashews (2 F)

Day Twenty
Breakfast
Oat bran Flaxseed Muffin *recipe* (2 C) (1 F)
4 ounces fruit juice (1 C)
Snack
¾ cup *Good Friends* (1 C)
6 almonds (1 F)
Lunch
2 slices whole-wheat pita bread (2 C)
3 ounces turkey (3 P)
1 slice low-fat cheese (1 P)
1 Tbsp. light mayonnaise (1 F)
2 Tbsp. avocado (1 F)
Lettuce, tomatoes, sprouts
1 fruit (1 C)
Snack
Hummus *recipe* (1 C) (1 P)
1 cup vegetables to dip
6 whole-grain crackers (1 C)
Dinner
Fried Flounder *recipe* (6 P) (1 C)
Cauliflower Casserole *recipe* (1 C)(1 F)
Snack
1 fruit (1 C)
12 almonds (2 F)

Xtra effort gives you the results you want!

Day Twenty-One

Breakfast

1 cup cooked oatmeal made with water (2 C)
4 walnuts, chopped (2 F)
1 fruit (1 C)

Lunch

Large salad (1 C)
½ cup chickpeas (1 C) (1 P)
3 ounces shrimp (3 P)
1 ounce goat cheese (1 P)
10 low-sodium olives (1 F)
2 Tbsp. light dressing (1 F)
2 Tbsp. avocado (1 F)
6 whole-grain crackers (1 C)

Snack

Low-fat spinach dip *recipe* (1 C)
1 cup vegetables to dip
6 whole-grain crackers (1 C)

Dinner

Salmon Teriyaki, Kasha and Vegetables *recipe* (6 P) (3 C)

Snack

Sugar-free Jell-O (free)
1 fruit (1 C)
12 cashews (2 F)

Day Twenty-Two

Breakfast

2 slices toast (2 C)
½ cup low-fat cottage cheese (2 P)

Snack

1 light fruit yogurt (1 C) (1 P)
12 almonds (2 F)

Lunch

Large salad (1 C)
2 tsp. olive oil plus vinegar (2 F)
½ cup chickpeas (1 C) (1 P)
2 ounces goat cheese (2 P)
3 ounces fish (3 P)

Snack

Fruit shake made with ¾ cup berries, 4 ounces skim milk, ½ ripe banana and ice (2 C)

Dinner

1 hamburger bun (2 C)
1 Vegetable Burger (2 P)
Medium potato (baked as fries) *recipe* (2 C)
Homemade coleslaw *recipe* (1 F)

Snack

1 fruits (1 C)
12 almonds (2 F)

It's time for your weekly weigh-in. See how much you've already accomplished!

Day Twenty-Three
Breakfast
High-fiber muffin *recipe*
(1 C) (1 F)
4 ounces fruit juice (1 C)
Snack
1 fruit (1 C)
6 almonds (1 F)
Lunch
2 slices whole-grain bread (2 C)
3 ounces turkey (3 P)
1 slice low-fat cheese (1 P)
Lettuce and tomato
Snack
6 animal crackers (1 C)
25-calorie fat-free hot cocoa
(free)
Dinner
6 ounces grilled fish (6 P)
1 cup cooked kasha (2 C)
3 cups cooked broccoli (2 C)
sautéed in
1 Tbsp. olive oil (3 F)
Snack
1 cup low-fat ice cream
(2 C) (1 F) (1 P)
6 cashews (1 F)

Day Twenty-Four
Breakfast
1 whole-wheat bagel (4 C)
1 poached egg (1 P) (1 F)
1 slice low-fat cheese (1 P)
Lunch
Portabella Mushroom Sandwich
recipe (1 C) (2 P)
1 fruit (1 C)
Snack
¾ cup Kashi's *Good Friends*
cereal (1 C)
3 dried apricots (1 C)
25- fat-free hot cocoa (free)
Dinner
5 ounces grilled salmon (5 P)
Potato-Zucchini Cake *recipe*
(1 P) (2 C) (2 F)
Snack
1 cup low-fat ice cream
(2 C) (1 F) (1 P)
3 walnuts (3 F)

*Be sure to use fluids, fiber and vegetables
to fill yourself up with minimal calories!*

Day Twenty-Five	*Day Twenty-Six*
Breakfast	**Breakfast**
1 ½ cups Kashi's *Good Friends* cereal (2 C)	2 slices whole-wheat bread (2 C)
1 cup skim milk (1 C) (1 P)	½ cup cottage cheese (2 P)
1 fruit (1 C)	**Snack**
1 poached egg (1 P) (1 F)	1 fruit (1 C)
Lunch	6 almonds (1 F)
Garden burger (2 P)	**Lunch**
1 slice low-fat cheese (1 P)	2 slices whole-wheat bread (2 C)
1 hamburger bun (2 C)	2 ounces tuna (2 P)
Broccoli sprouts	Broccoli sprouts
2 Tbsp. avocado (1 F)	1 Tbsp. light mayonnaise (1 F)
Snack	**Snack**
1 fruit (1 C)	6 – 8 cups popcorn (2 C)
12 cashews (2 F)	**Dinner**
Dinner	6 ounces fish, poultry, or lean meat, baked (6 P)
6 ounces chicken (6 P)	Tabouleh *recipe* (1 C) (1 F)
1 large sweet potato (baked as chips) *recipe* (3 C)	3 cups steamed broccoli (2 C)
1 ½ cups cooked vegetables, steamed (1 C)	6 almonds slivered on broccoli (1 F)
Snack	**Snack**
1 fruit (1 C)	1 cup low-fat ice cream (2 C) (1 F) (1 P)
12 almonds and 2 walnuts (3 F)	4 walnuts (2 F)

Yes!
It can be done. You owe it to yourself.
You are what you choose to be.

Day Twenty-Seven
Breakfast
2-egg omelet (2 P) (2 F)
2 tsp. canola oil (to make omelet) (2 F)
Tomatoes and spinach (free)
2 slices low-fat cheese (2 P)
½ large pumpernickel bagel (2 C)
1 Tbsp. light whipped butter (1 F)
Lunch
Large salad (1 C)
2 Tbsp. light dressing (1 F)
3 ounces fish (3 P)
1 cup chickpeas (2 C) (2 P)
Snack
¾ cup Kashi's *Good Friends* cereal (1 C)
6 almonds (1 F)
Dinner
Eggplant Parmigiana Hero (5 C) with 2 slices low-fat cheese (2 P)
Snack
1 crepe, ½ banana and ¼ cup berries (1 C)
2 Tbsp. light whipped cream (free)

Day Twenty-Eight
Breakfast
1 whole-wheat bagel (4 C)
2 slices Jarlsberg light cheese (2 P)
1 poached egg (1 P) (1 F)
2 slices tomato
Lunch
Spinach Pie *recipe* (2 P) (1 C) (1F)
Snack
1 light fruit yogurt (1 C) (1 P)
¾ cup Kashi's *Good Friends* cereal (1 C)
Dinner
Large salad (1 C)
2 Tbsp. light dressing (1 F)
2 ounces shredded cheese (2 P)
Shrimp, Vegetable, and Pasta Casserole *recipe* (2 C) (3 P) (2 F)
Snack
12 almonds (2 F)
2 fruits (2 C)

It's time for your weekly weigh-in. See how much you've already accomplished!

Day Twenty-Nine	**Day Thirty**
Breakfast	**Breakfast**
½ cup low-fat cottage cheese (2 P)	Fruit shake: blend 1 ripe banana with ¾ cup berries and 8 ounces low-fat milk (3 C) (1 P)
1 whole-wheat English muffin (2 C)	1 slice whole-wheat toast (1 C)
1 fruit (1 C)	1 slice low-fat cheese (1 P)
Lunch	2 poached eggs (2 P) (2 F)
Large salad (1 C)	**Lunch**
2 Tbsp. light dressing (1 F)	Large salad (1 C)
3 ounces shrimp (3 P)	2 Tbsp. light dressing (1 F)
1 ounce goat cheese (1 P)	3 ounces chicken, baked (3 P)
½ cup chickpeas (1 C) (1 P)	1 slice low-fat cheese (1 P)
10 peanuts (1 F)	10 low-sodium olives (1 F)
Snack	6 whole-grain crackers (1 C)
1 light fruit yogurt (1 C) (1 P)	**Snack**
12 pistachio nuts (2 F)	1 light fruit yogurt (1 C) (1 P)
Dinner	6 almonds (1 F)
Vegetable Chow Mein *recipe* (2 C) (1 F)	**Dinner**
add 3 ounces of chicken or shrimp (3 P)	Veggie Mexican *recipe* (3 C) (2 P) (1 F)
Snack	**Snack**
2 Applesauce-Oatmeal Cookies *recipe* (4 C) (2 F)	6 cashews (1 F)
25-calorie fat-free hot cocoa (free)	2 fruits (2 C)
	Sugar-free Jell-O (free)

Zero excuses!

Chapter Four: Easy Preparations

Soups and Salads

Avocado, Shrimp, Roasted Garlic and Walnut Salad

(serves 2)

2 cups of salad greens
¼ small diced avocado
¼ Bermuda onion diced
4 walnuts, chopped
6 ounces of medium prepared shrimp
2 tsp. olive oil
2 Tbsp. vinegar
1 large tomato, diced
4 roasted garlic cloves (steam garlic in microwave for 1-2 minutes covered)
Pepper to taste

Mix together and enjoy!

Per Serving Count	
Carbohydrate	1
Protein	3
Fat	3

Caesar Salad

(serves 4)

1 head of Romaine lettuce
1 Tbsp. Anchovy paste
1 clove garlic smashed
1 tsp. dry mustard
½ cup Parmesan cheese
¼ cup lemon juice
1/8 cup water
2 Tbsp. olive oil
Pepper to taste

Combine oil, lemon juice, water, mustard, garlic, anchovy paste, Parmesan cheese and pepper. Pour over romaine lettuce.

Per serving count:	
Carbohydrate	1
Protein	1
Fat	2

Leaf and Nut Salad

(serves one)

Romaine lettuce, tomatoes, cucumbers, mushrooms, peppers, etc. Mix together in a large bowl. Then choose two of the following:
2 walnuts, chopped
6 pecans, chopped
6 almonds, chopped
2 Tbsp. avocado
10 low-sodium black olives

3 ounces of lean protein (steamed or grilled shrimp/scallops or other fish, tofu or poultry serving that is steamed, broiled or baked)

½ cup chickpeas or ½ cup of plain bean of your choice

2 Tbsp. light-dressing or vinaigrette or 1 tsp. olive oil plus vinegar

Per Serving Count	
Carbohydrate	2
Protein	3
Fat	3

Marinated Bean and Vegetable Salad

(serves 8)

1 pound cut green beans (frozen, fresh or low-sodium can)
1 pound kidney beans (canned and rinsed)
1 can artichoke hearts or Hearts of Palm (rinsed and chopped)
1 can (6 ounces dry weight) low-sodium black olives
1 small red thinly-sliced onion
1 16-ounce can chickpeas (rinsed)
2 ounces pimentos, chopped
¼ cup chopped fresh parsley
1 Tbsp. chopped scallions or chives

Dressing:
¼ cup olive oil
¼ cup vinegar
1 tsp. tarragon
Salt and pepper to taste
1 clove garlic minced
Pinch of cayenne pepper (optional)

Mix all the above together and enjoy!

Per Serving Count	
Carbohydrate	1
Protein	1
Fat	2

Salad Vinaigrette Dressing

(2 Tbsp. per serving)

In a cruet, mix ½ cup balsamic vinegar and ¼ cup of olive, pumpkin or walnut oil. Add a pinch of basil, pepper, lemon juice, mustard powder and the rest with water (about 1/4 cruet) and shake. That's it!

Per Serving Count	
Carbohydrate	0
Protein	0
Fat	1.5

Barley Vegetable Soup

(serves 4)

½ cup pearl barley
3 cans (10 ¾ ounce) reduced-fat/low-sodium chicken broth
1 stalk celery, cut into 1-inch slices
1 bay leaf
Pepper to taste
3 carrots, sliced
½ zucchini, sliced
½ cup onion, chopped
10 ounces frozen chopped spinach

Place barley, chicken stock, onions, carrots, celery, zucchini, spinach and bay leaf in a large soup pot and bring to a boil. Reduce heat, cover, and simmer for about one hour or until barley and vegetables are tender.

Per Serving Count	
Carbohydrate	1
Protein	0
Fat	0

Bean Soup with Kale

(serves 8)

1 Tbsp. olive oil
8 large garlic cloves, crushed or minced
1 medium onion, chopped
4 cups chopped raw kale or 10 ounces frozen chopped kale (squeeze out the water)
4 cups low-fat, low-sodium chicken or vegetable broth
2 15-ounce cans of white beans such as cannelloni or navy beans (about 3 cups)
4 plum tomatoes, chopped
2 tsp. dried Italian herb seasoning (or 1 tsp. each of dried thyme and rosemary)
Salt and pepper to taste
1 cup chopped parsley

In a large pot, heat olive oil. Add garlic and onion; sauté until soft. Add kale and sauté, stirring, until wilted. Add 3 cups of broth, 2 cups of beans, and the tomato, herbs, salt and pepper and simmer for 5 minutes.

In a blender or food processor, mix the remaining beans and broth until smooth. Stir into soup to thicken. Simmer 15 minutes. Ladle into bowls; sprinkle with chopped parsley.

Per Serving Count	
Carbohydrate	1
Protein	1
Fat	.5

Cauliflower Soup

(serves 4)

1 large head cauliflower
1 can fat-free, low-sodium chicken broth (10 ounces)
2 stalks celery, diced
2 scallions (green onions), sliced
1 tsp. olive oil
2 Tbsp. white flour
1-2 cups water

Remove and discard cauliflower stems. Steam flowerets until tender and set aside 1 cup of cauliflower flowerets. Puree cauliflower (all except the 1 cup put aside) with chicken broth in blender. Set aside. In a 10-inch skillet sauté the celery and green onions in oil until tender. Reduce heat to medium and stir in flour. Stir in cauliflower puree. Slowly mix in one cup of water, stirring constantly until soup thickens. If soup is too thick, stir in remaining water, ¼ cup at a time. Continue cooking until warmed through. Cut reserved flowerets into bite-sized pieces, add to soup and serve.

Per Serving Count	
Carbohydrate	1
Protein	0
Fat	0

Chicken and Vegetable Soup

(serves 14)

1-2 pounds of skinless/boneless chicken breasts/thighs
Frozen bag of chopped onions
10 oz. frozen box of chopped spinach
10 oz. frozen box of chopped broccoli
10 oz. frozen box of Brussels sprouts
10 oz. frozen box of mixed vegetables
10 garlic cloves
3 leek stalks, chopped
Dill and pepper to taste
Kosher salt to taste if needed
7 quarts of water (28 cups)

Use a large soup pot and place all ingredients in the water. Boil to cook vegetables until soft and chicken is fully done (no pink).

Per Serving Count	
Carbohydrate	3
Protein	1-2
Fat	0

Cream of Broccoli Soup

(serves 4)

1 Tbsp. olive oil
½ cup diced onion
1 - 10 ounce package frozen chopped broccoli
½ tsp. salt
1 bay leaf
1 tsp. flour
12 ounce can of evaporated skim milk
½ cup canned low-sodium fat-free chicken broth

In a 10-inch skillet sauté onion in oil until brown. Microwave broccoli until soft, then add it to the onion mixture along with salt and bay leaf. Sprinkle flour on top of mixture and stir to combine. Continue stirring and add milk and broth until it boils. Reduce heat and simmer until mixture thickens. Discard bay leaf. Transfer ½ of mixture and blend until smooth. Then add the other ½ and combine. Serve.

Per Serving Count	
Carbohydrate	1
Protein	0
Fat	1

Cream of Broccoli Soup with Oats à la Patty
(serves 2)

1 medium onion, diced
1 tsp. light sesame oil
4 cups water
4 broccoli stalks
½ tsp. salt
½ cup uncooked rolled oats
Scallions or croutons to garnish

Sauté onion in oil until brown. Add it to a medium-sized pot of 4 cups of water. Cut broccoli into small chunks. Add broccoli, salt, and oats to water. Bring to boil, lower heat, and simmer for about 30 minutes, until broccoli is very soft. Put all ingredients in a blender or food processor and blend until smooth. Garnish with scallions before serving.

Per Serving Count	
Carbohydrate	1
Protein	0
Fat	1

Cream of Spinach Soup

(serves 4)

1 Tbsp. olive oil
1 cup diced onions
2 chicken bouillon
1 Tbsp. flour
3 cups skim milk
1 10-ounce package of frozen chopped spinach microwave until soft and drained

In a 1 ½-quart saucepan sauté the onions in oil. Sprinkle flour on top and stir quickly to combine; cook, stirring constantly for 1 minute. Continue stirring and gradually add milk and bouillon and bring to a boil. Reduce heat and simmer, stirring, until mixture thickens. Stir in cooked spinach and remove from heat.

Pour soup into blender or food processor and blend until smooth.

Per Serving Count	
Carbohydrate	1
Protein	1
Fat	1

Lentil and Vegetable Soup
(serves 4)

1 Tbsp. olive oil
2/3 cup diced celery
1/3 cup diced onions
1/3 cup diced carrots
½ cup chopped zucchini (buy frozen and sliced)
½ cup chopped broccoli (buy frozen)
½ cup chopped spinach (buy frozen)
1 Tbsp. minced garlic
2 quarts vegetable stock (buy pre-made - it's easier!)
Add more water if necessary
1 ¼ cup dry brown lentils
2 tsp. mustard
2 tsp. red wine vinegar
Salt and pepper to taste

Heat oil in a saucepan over medium heat. Sauté celery, onions, carrots, zucchini, broccoli, spinach, and garlic until onions are translucent. Add vegetable stock and lentils. Cook uncovered until lentils are just tender but not too soft. Before serving, add mustard, vinegar, salt and pepper.

Per Serving Count	
Carbohydrate	2
Protein	2
Fat	1

Potato Leek Soup

(serves 4)

1 Tbsp. olive oil
1 ½ cups chopped leeks (white part only)
2 cloves garlic chopped finely
2 cans reduced sodium chicken broth (3½ cups)
4 medium sized potatoes, peeled and cubed
¼ tsp. celery seed
¼ tsp. pepper
¼ tsp. salt
¾ cup skim milk, skim plus, 1% milk
1 Tbsp. all-purpose flour
11-ounce can of whole kernel corn, no salt added, drained

In a 2-quart saucepan heat oil and add leeks, stirring often, for 4 minutes. Add garlic; cook, stirring, for 30 seconds. Add broth, potatoes, corn, celery seed, pepper, and salt. Bring to a boil. Reduce heat; cover and simmer until vegetables are tender about 15 minutes. Let cool for 10 minutes. Remove 1½ cups potato and leek mixture. In a blender/food processor, process remaining soup until smooth. Pour the mixture back into the saucepan. Whisk together milk and flour until blended. Stir in soup, return to saucepan and bring to a boil. Reduce heat and stir often until slightly thickened (2 minutes). Stir in corn and reserved potato-leek mixture. Heat through and serve immediately.

Per Serving Count	
Carbohydrate	3
Protein	0
Fat	1

Savory Split Pea Soup

(serves 4)

1 Tbsp. olive oil
2 cups chopped onion
½ cup chopped celery
1 clove garlic, pressed or finely chopped
1/8 tsp. ground red pepper
2 cans reduced sodium chicken broth (3 ½ cups)
½ cup water
4 – 5 whole large carrots
1-cup green split peas

In a 4-quart saucepan, heat oil over medium heat. Add onion and celery and stir often for about 5 minutes. Add garlic and red pepper and continue stirring for 30 seconds. Add broth, water, carrots, peas, and bay leaf. Bring to a boil. Reduce heat; cover and simmer until split peas are tender, about 1 hour. Remove from heat and cool for 10 minutes. Remove carrots and discard bay leaf. Cool carrots slightly and chop; set aside. Blend mixture in blender or food processor and add in chopped carrots after the mixture is smooth.

Per Serving Count	
Carbohydrate	1
Protein	1
Fat	1

Shrimp and Corn Chowder

(serves 4)

3 cups low-sodium chicken broth
4 medium red potatoes
1 16-ounce package frozen white corn, thawed
1 bunch chopped scallions
½ pound thawed shrimp, peeled, de-veined, and cut into ½ inch pieces
¼ cup fat free sour cream or evaporated skim milk
1 Tbsp. lemon juice

In a 4-quart saucepan, boil broth and potatoes for 5 minutes. Add corn and white portion of scallion; simmer 8 minutes. Remove 2 cups; puree in a blender. Return to pot; stir in shrimp. Cook until bright pink; stir in fat-free sour cream or evaporated skim milk, lemon juice and scallion greens. Season with salt and pepper.

Per Serving Count	
Carbohydrate	3
Protein	2
Fat	0

Vegetable Soup

(serves 14)

Frozen bag of chopped onions
10 oz. frozen box of chopped spinach
10 oz. frozen box of chopped broccoli
10 oz. frozen box of Brussels sprouts
10 oz. frozen box of mixed vegetables
10 garlic cloves
3 leek stalks chopped
Dill and pepper
Use either *Streits* soup mix or 3 quarts low-sodium vegetable broth and 4 quarts of water, or use only 7 quarts of water (28 cups)
Added salt if needed

In a large soup pot place ingredients in water or ½ water and ½ low-sodium broth mixture. Allow all to boil and cook until ready.

Per Serving Count	
Carbohydrate	1
Protein	0
Fat	0

Appetizers

Baked Clam Dip

(serves 3)

1 Tbsp. olive oil
1 medium chopped onion
1 stalk celery chopped
3 cloves garlic chopped
2 6 1/2-ounce cans of chopped clams, drained
¾ cup breadcrumbs, seasoned
2 Tbsp. grated Parmesan cheese (optional)

Sauté garlic, celery, and onion in the olive oil until brown. Add the chopped clams and breadcrumbs and stir. Bake in an uncovered dish at 350 degrees for 20 minutes.

Enjoy with semolina bread or crackers.

Per Serving Count	
Carbohydrate	1
Protein	4
Fat	1

Marci Page Sloane MS, RD, LD/N, CDE

Black Bean and Corn Dip

(serves 4)

One 16-ounce can of black beans, drained and rinsed
One 11-ounce canned corn with no salt added, drained
½ cup salsa
2 Tbsp. lime juice
1 Tbsp. chopped fresh cilantro or 1 tsp. dry coriander
¼ tsp. cumin
¼ tsp. red pepper sauce (Tabasco)

Combine black beans and corn with salsa, lime juice, cilantro, cumin, and red pepper sauce. Mash or blend together. Serve with baked tortilla chips or raw vegetables.

Optional: Bake Pepper Jack or Monterey Jack low-fat cheese on top (each slice: 1 P additional).

Per Serving Count	
Carbohydrate	2
Protein	1
Fat	0

Eggplant Caponata á la Lois

(serves 6)

2 medium eggplants
1 large onion, diced
2 stalks celery, diced
1 red pepper, diced
1 yellow pepper, diced
1 large can no-salt diced tomatoes
3 cloves garlic
1 cup low-sodium black olives and green olives with pimentos, halved
2 Tbsp. vinegar
¼ cup olive oil

Cube unpeeled eggplant and sauté 10 minutes in olive oil until soft. Remove from skillet. Sauté onion, celery, and peppers in olive oil. Add tomatoes, garlic. Sauté 15 minutes. Add olives and vinegar and mix all together. May be served hot or cold.

Per Serving Count	
Carbohydrate	1
Protein	0
Fat	3

Eggplant Dip
(serves 3)

One eggplant
One large onion, diced
1/8 –1/4 cup lemon juice to taste
1 Tbsp. garlic powder to taste
1 Tbsp. olive oil

Poke holes in eggplant and bake or microwave until it collapses. Dice a large onion. Peel and chop eggplant and add onion, garlic, oil and lemon juice.

This is a great dip to use with whole-grain crackers (without hydrogenated fats) or raw vegetables.

Per Serving Count	
Carbohydrate	1
Protein	0
Fat	1

Guacamole Dip

(serves 6)

2 medium ripe avocados
1 medium onion
1 medium tomato
1 tsp. cumin (or to taste)
1 tsp. cayenne pepper to taste
Hot sauce to taste

Mash avocados and add diced onion and diced tomato. Add spices and dig in with some baked tortilla chips (15 chips per person).

Per Serving Count	
Carbohydrate	1
Protein	0
Fat	3

Hummus

(serves 4)

1 16-ounce can of garbanzo beans (chickpeas) rinsed and drained
1 vegetable bouillon cube
2 cups of water
½ tsp. garlic powder or more to taste
¼ cup diced red onion
1 tsp. dried parsley
3 Tbsp. lemon juice

Boil chickpeas in the water and bouillon. Strain the water and set aside. Add garlic, onion, parsley, and lemon juice and mash the beans finely. Add broth that had been set aside for desired consistency.

Enjoy with non-hydrogenated crackers or raw vegetables.

Per Serving Count	
Carbohydrate	1
Protein	1
Fat	0

Low-fat Spinach Dip

(serves 4)

16 ounces non-fat sour cream
1 Tbsp. reduced-fat mayonnaise
10 ounces frozen chopped spinach. Microwave and drain
Knorr's Vegetable Soup mix

Mix all the above ingredients together and allow to chill
for 1-2 hours. Eat with vegetables or non-hydrogenated
crackers.

Per Serving Count	
Carbohydrate	1
Protein	0
Fat	0

Vegetarian Chopped Liver

(serves 4)

2 cups frozen French-style green beans, microwave until soft
4 hard-boiled whole eggs
1 large onion, diced
10 chopped walnuts
1 Tbsp. olive oil
Salt and pepper to taste

Sauté onion in olive oil and add the rest of the ingredients. Put through a food processor or grinder. Serve with whole grain, non-hydrogenated crackers. (6 crackers: add 1 C)

Per Serving Count	
Carbohydrate	1
Protein	1
Fat	2

Side Dishes

Bean Sprouts and Sesame Oil

(serves 4)

2 10-ounce packages fresh bean sprouts
¼ tsp. dry mustard
½ cup red wine vinegar
2 Tbsp. brown sugar
½ cup light soy sauce
1 Tbsp. sesame oil

Boil bean sprouts in water. When soft, rinse in cool water and drain. Whisk together remaining ingredients. Toss and refrigerate for about ½ hour.

Per Serving Count	
Carbohydrate	1
Protein	0
Fat	1

Brussels Sprouts

(serves 4)

2 Tbsp. olive oil
1/8 cup minced cloves of garlic in water
2 10-ounce frozen boxes of Brussels sprouts, microwave until soft and drain

Stir-fry together!

Per Serving Count	
Carbohydrate	.5
Protein	0
Fat	2

Bulgur Pilaf

(serves 4)

1 cup bulgur: dry, cracked, unseasoned
1 tsp. salt (optional)
1 large onion, chopped
1 red, yellow or green pepper, chopped
2 tsp. of olive oil
2 low-sodium chicken/vegetable bouillon cubes
2 cups boiling water

Sauté onion and pepper in olive oil. Add the bulgur and stir.
Add water and bouillon cubes, stir and cover and simmer
until ready.

Per Serving Count	
Carbohydrate	1
Protein	0
Fat	1

Cauliflower Casserole

(serves 4)

1 head cauliflower
Water for steaming
Salt and pepper to taste
1 medium diced onion
1 Tbsp. olive oil
1 egg, beaten, or 2 egg whites
¼ cup (4 Tbsp.) breadcrumbs
1 large diced zucchini

Wash and steam cauliflower well (using only florets). Drain fluid and mash. Sauté onion and zucchini in a pan with oil. Combine sautéed mixture with mashed cauliflower and put in casserole dish. Add salt and pepper to taste. Mix in beaten egg and combine. Sprinkle ¼ cup breadcrumbs on top. Bake in oven at 350 degrees for about 20-30 minutes or until brown.

Per Serving Count	
Carbohydrate	1
Protein	0
Fat	1

Cole Slaw

(serves 8)

Shredded red cabbage and white angel hair cabbage
Shredded carrots
Mix in Hellmann's low-fat/light mayonnaise (1/4 cup)
Add 1/8 cup white vinegar
Add salt, pepper and garlic powder to taste

Let sit in refrigerator for ½- 1 hour

Per Serving Count	
Carbohydrate	-
Protein	-
Fat	1

French Fried Potatoes

(each 6-ounce medium potato serves one)

Microwave white potatoes, red potatoes or Yukon gold potatoes for 3 minutes. When semi-soft, slice into fries. Spray *Pam* (non-stick spray) on a cookie sheet under and over the potatoes. Add spices if you like (garlic, onion powder, cayenne pepper, etc). Bake at 350 degrees for about 20 minutes or until as crispy as you would like them.

Per Serving Count	
Carbohydrate	2
Protein	0
Fat	0

Peanut Noodles

(serves 2)

1 Tbsp. canola oil
2 tsp. minced fresh ginger
2 cloves garlic, minced
1 Tbsp. low-sodium soy sauce
4 tsp. rice vinegar
½ tsp. red-pepper flakes or Asian chili sauce
1/3 cup natural peanut butter
½ cup lower-sodium non-fat chicken broth
½ tsp. salt
2 cups dry noodles (4 cups cooked) preferably soba
topped with ¼ cup bean sprouts
Add 3 ounces shrimp, chicken or tofu for each serving

Heat oil over medium-high heat in a saucepan. Add ginger and garlic; cook, stirring, for two minutes. Add soy sauce, vinegar, chili sauce or red peppers, peanut butter, broth and salt; cook, stirring, until peanut butter is dissolved. Simmer over low heat for 7 minutes, until thick and smooth. Add shrimp or tofu if desired and cook for 4 minutes.

Per Serving Count	
Carbohydrate	4
Protein	4
Fat	1

Portabella Mushroom Sandwich

(serves two)

2 large mushroom caps, cleaned
Tomato, thickly sliced
Bermuda onion, thickly sliced
Eggplant, thickly sliced
Jarlsberg light cheese or Veggie Soy Mozzarella (or other low-fat cheese)

Take 2 large mushroom caps, wash and peel
Place a thick slice of tomato, onion and eggplant on each cap.
Bake until soft.
Drain fluid.
Put slice of cheese on top and melt until brown in oven 250 degrees or toaster oven (top brown).

Per Serving Count	
Carbohydrate	1
Protein	2
Fat	0

Potato-Zucchini Cake

(serves 4)

2 Tbsp. olive oil
1 onion, chopped
1 clove garlic, minced
2 large potatoes, grated
1 large zucchini, grated
2 Tbsp. chopped fresh dill
1 tsp. salt
¼ tsp. pepper
1 egg
½ grated Parmesan cheese

In large skillet heat, 1 Tbsp. oil over medium heat. Add onion and garlic. Cook until softened, about 8 minutes, and set aside. In a large bowl, combine potatoes, zucchini, dill, salt, and pepper. Stir in egg. In the same skillet, heat remaining oil over medium high heat. Add the vegetable mixture, pressing down to flatten. Cook until bottom browns, 5 minutes. When brown, turn over and brown other side. Sprinkle cheese on top when ready to serve.

Per Serving Count	
Carbohydrate	2
Protein	1
Fat	2

Stuffed Zucchini

(serves 2)

2 medium zucchini
1 small chopped onion
1 cup mushrooms, chopped
½ cup celery, chopped
1 fresh medium chopped tomato
1/2 cup breadcrumbs
1 egg or 2 egg whites
¼ cup Parmesan grated cheese
Paprika or turmeric

Cut zucchini in half lengthwise and scoop out pulp leaving ¼ inch shell. Chop the pulp. In a 1 ½ quart casserole, combine with onion, mushrooms, celery, and tomatoes, cover and microwave on high for 4-6 minutes or until tender, stirring once during cooling. Drain thoroughly. Add breadcrumbs, egg whites, and cheese. Mound ¼ of the filling in each zucchini shell and sprinkle with paprika or turmeric. Arrange the stuffed zucchini and cover before putting in the microwave. Microwave on high for 5-7 minutes or until filling is set and the zucchini is fork tender.

Per Serving Count	
Carbohydrate	2
Protein	2
Fat	0

Sweet Potato Chips

(1 medium sweet potato serves one)

Take a raw sweet potato and thinly slice. Spray *Pam* (non-stick spray) on a cookie sheet and bake at 350 degrees until brown.

Per Serving Count	
Carbohydrate	2
Protein	0
Fat	0

Tabouleh

(serves 4)

1 cup dry bulgur wheat
1 ½ cups water
Salt and pepper to taste
4 ripe plum tomatoes
2 scallions, diced
1 stalk celery
1 Tbsp. olive oil
10 sliced low-sodium black olives or green olives
3 Tbsp. lemon juice

Boil water and add bulgur. Cover and simmer until done. Chill. In another pan, sauté the tomatoes, scallions, and celery in olive oil. Add this mixture to the chilled bulgur in addition to the olives and lemon juice. Serve.

Per Serving Count	
Carbohydrate	1
Protein	0
Fat	1

Breads/Muffins

Corn Bread

(serves 12)

1 cup unbleached white flour
¾ cup cornmeal (stone-ground if possible)
2 Tbsp. sugar
1 Tbsp. plus 1 tsp. double-acting baking powder
1 tsp. salt
1 egg, beaten
1 cup low-fat milk
1/4 cup canola oil
Pam spray

Sift together all the dry ingredients in a bowl. In another bowl combine the milk, oil, beaten egg and add it to the flour mixture. Stir everything up well.

Spread the batter in a bread mold sprayed with non-stick spray and bake at 425 degrees for about 15-20 minutes or until it is lightly browned around the edges.

Per Serving Count	
Carbohydrate	1
Protein	0
Fat	1

Flaxseed Bread

(serves 8)

1 cup warm water
2 Tbsp. honey
1 package active dry yeast
1/3 cup soy flour
1/3 cup flaxseed meal
1 cup whole-wheat flour
½ tsp. salt
1 Tbsp. olive oil

Combine mixture and knead and place into a bread mold.
Bake at 375 degrees for 35 minutes.

Per Serving Count	
Carbohydrate	1
Protein	0
Fat	0

High-Fiber Muffins

(serves 12)

1 ¼ cups 100% rolled oats
1 cup unbleached soy or white flour
1 cup chopped apples (1 medium to large apple)
1/3 cup unprocessed bran
½ cup chopped walnuts
1 Tbsp. vanilla
1 Tbsp. cinnamon
1 Tbsp. baking powder
1 tsp. baking soda
½ cup skim or low-fat milk
¼ cup olive oil
¼ cup sugar
2 eggs or 4 egg whites or ½ cup egg substitutes

Mix all the above ingredients together. Spray *Pam* in a 12-muffin tray. Bake at 400 degrees for 15-20 minutes or until brown.

Per Serving Count	
Carbohydrate	1
Protein	0
Fat	1

Oat Bran Flaxseed Muffins

(serves 12)

1 ½ cups all-purpose flour
¾ cup flaxseed meal
¾ cup oat bran
2/3 cup brown sugar
2 tsp. baking soda
1 tsp. baking powder
½ tsp. salt
1 ½ tsp. cinnamon
½ tsp. nutmeg
2/3 cup unsweetened applesauce
1 cup chopped walnuts
¾ cup skim milk, skim plus, 1% milk
2 beaten eggs or 4 beaten egg whites
1 tsp. vanilla

Mix flour, flaxseed meal, bran, sugar, baking soda and powder, salt and spices in a bowl. Stir in applesauce and walnuts. Combine milk, beaten eggs, and vanilla. Pour liquid ingredients into dry ingredients. Stir until ingredients are moistened. Do not over mix! Fill cups ¾ full. Bake at 350 degrees for 15-20 minutes. Makes 12 muffins.

Per Serving Count	
Carbohydrate	2
Protein	0
Fat	1

Pumpkin and Wheat Bran Bread

(serves 12)

2 cups of pumpkin (use canned 100% pumpkin only)
2 cups unprocessed wheat bran
3 eggs (6 egg whites)
1 cup evaporated skim milk
1 cup unsweetened or natural applesauce
¼ cup brown sugar
1 ½ cups of whole-wheat flour
1 cup white or soy flour
1 Tbsp. baking powder
1 tsp. baking soda
1 Tbsp. cinnamon
1 Tbsp. nutmeg
1 Tbsp. ground ginger
1 Tbsp. ground cloves or Allspice
1 Tbsp. vanilla
1 cup chopped walnuts

In a large mixing bowl, combine the pumpkin, egg, milk, sugar and applesauce. In a separate bowl, whisk together the flour, wheat bran, baking powder, baking soda, walnuts, cinnamon and other spices including vanilla. Combine both wet and dry ingredients. Coat bread or muffin tin with Pam spray. Pour in mixture and bake on 350 degrees for approximately 30 minutes or until brown and a toothpick inserted in the center of the bread or muffin comes out clean.

Per Serving Count	
Carbohydrate	2
Protein	.5
Fat	1

Entrees

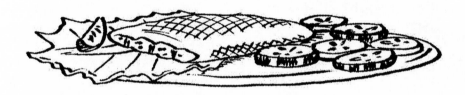

Eggplant Lasagna

(serves 4)

1 eggplant
Classico Tomato and Basil Sauce
1 pint each fat-free and low-fat ricotta cheese
2 large zucchini, shredded
1 large onion, shredded
Seasoned breadcrumbs
1 egg, beaten

Peel and slice eggplant. Coat each slice with egg and breadcrumbs. In Pyrex dish cover bottom with tomato sauce. Line the coated eggplant (about four slices over sauce). Add shredded zucchini and onion over mixture. Layer mixture of fat-free and low-fat ricotta cheese. Repeat layering with sauce, etc. No more than four layers of eggplant!

Per Serving Count	
Carbohydrate	2
Protein	4
Fat	0

Eggplant Parmigiana Hero

(serves 2)

Large semolina or whole-wheat hero roll
1 wide eggplant
1 cup *Classico* or *Five Brothers* tomato sauce
Garlic and basil to taste

Wash and peel eggplant and slice to make large, thin slices. Layer on plate and cover. Microwave for five minutes or until very tender. Heat a cup of tomato sauce while you are toasting bread. Line each roll with eggplant and pour the sauce over it. No cheese necessary! (If you absolutely must use cheese, try mozzarella veggie slices, 2 Tbsp. grated Parmesan or part skim milk cheese (each ounce = 1 P).

Per Serving Count	
Carbohydrate	5
Protein	0
Fat	0

"Fried" Fish

(serves 2)

12-ounce flounder filet
¼ cup seasoned breadcrumbs
¼ cup milk
Non-stick spray

Coat fish in milk, and sprinkle breadcrumbs all over piece of fish. Spray *Pam* over fish (this allows it to brown when you bake it in the oven) and bake on 350 degrees for about 15-20 minutes.

Per Serving Count	
Carbohydrate	1
Protein	6
Fat	0

Poached Salmon

(serves 2)

12-ounce "wild" salmon without skin, cut into 2 pieces
1 large onion, diced
1 large tomato, diced
Juice from one lemon
Minced garlic to taste
1 Tbsp. dry dill

Take onion and tomato and line microwaveable dish with them. Place salmon over onion and tomato. Use lemon juice and other spices over fish. Cover and microwave for approximately 5 minutes or until done.

Per Serving Count	
Carbohydrate	.5
Protein	6
Fat	0

Salmon Teriyaki with Kasha and Vegetables

(serves 2)

2 6-ounce pieces of salmon filet
1 cup dry whole-granulation kasha
2 cups low-sodium vegetable broth
3 Tbsp. light teriyaki sauce
1 cup broccoli
1 cup spinach
1 diced onion
2 garlic cloves

Drizzle salmon filet with light teriyaki sauce and add sliced garlic cloves. Bake at 350 degrees until done.

Prepare kasha as you would rice: boil the low-sodium vegetable broth and add kasha then simmer until soft. When most of the broth is absorbed and the kasha is almost done, add vegetables until they are soft so they pick up the flavor of the broth and kasha. This mixture allows the vegetables and kasha to have a fabulous taste and it's easy in this one-pot meal!

Per Serving Count	
Carbohydrate	3
Protein	6
Fat	0

Scallops and Broccoli

(serves 2)

10 sea scallops
2 cups broccoli
3 cloves garlic
1 large onion
1 large tomato
1 Tbsp. olive oil

Sauté onion, garlic and tomato in olive oil. Pan-fry scallops until cooked. Add broccoli until done to taste. Put scallops and broccoli over sautéed items and serve.

Per Serving Count	
Carbohydrate	1
Protein	3
Fat	1

Shrimp, Tomato, Spinach and Feta

(serves 2)

2 Tbsp. olive oil
6 ounces of large shrimp (de-veined and cleaned)
3 cups raw spinach leaves
6 garlic cloves, sliced
1 large onion, diced
3 plum tomatoes, diced
½ cup Feta cheese, crumbled
Pepper to taste

Sauté garlic, onion and tomatoes in olive oil. When brown, add shrimp. When shrimp are cooked, add spinach leaves and cover. Top with feta cheese and pepper.

Per Serving Count	
Carbohydrate	1
Protein	4
Fat	1

Shrimp, Veggie and Pasta Casserole

(serves 4)

4 ounces part-skim mozzarella, shredded, or mozzarella veggie slices, shredded
1 medium onion, chopped
1 small yellow squash, diced
½ cup cauliflower
½ cup broccoli
1 cup spinach (fresh leaves)
3 large cloves garlic, diced
2 Tbsp. olive oil
12 ounces of large shrimp
½ tsp. basil
1/8 tsp. oregano
1/8 tsp. pepper
2 cups dry whole-wheat or white penne pasta (4 cups cooked)

Sauté onion and garlic in olive oil. When sizzle begins, add other vegetables (excluding spinach), and cover. Cook for 3–5 minutes on low heat, stirring occasionally. Add shrimp. Cook covered for 5 more minutes. Add seasoning. Mix and cover for 1-2 minutes. Add spinach and stir. Add this mixture to 4 cups of cooked penne pasta. Cover with shredded cheese.

Per Serving Count	
Carbohydrate	2
Protein	3
Fat	2

Spinach Pie

(serves 8)

4 10-ounce packages frozen chopped spinach
Filo leaves (Greek dough leaves)
Medium onion
1 egg
Pam cooking spray
3 Tbsp. melted butter
Pepper
1 package Feta cheese

Microwave spinach and drain very, very well. Squeeze out any excess water. Beat egg and add it to spinach. Grate onion and add to mixture. Crumble cheese and add to mixture along with pepper.

Spray bottom and sides of lasagna size pan with *Pam* cooking spray. Place five filo leaves on the bottom of the pan. Add all of mixture. Add five more leaves on top. (You may have to fold leaves in half. In this case, use five. If you do not double them, use 10 sheets each on top and bottom. Brush melted butter across top of spinach pie (the top layer of filo leaves). Bake at 350 degrees for about 30-45 minutes until slightly brown.

Per Serving Count	
Carbohydrate	1
Protein	2
Fat	1

Steamed Flounder and Black Beans

(2 servings)

1 Tbsp. olive oil
1 16-ounce can black beans, rinsed and drained
10 ounces flounder
1 large tomato
1 large onion
¼ cup Feta, blue or Gorgonzola cheese
3 garlic cloves sliced
1 bag of fresh spinach

Sauté onions and garlic in olive oil. Add tomatoes and spinach and beans and let cook until all flavors are incorporated. Add flounder fish on top of mixture and let cook until done. Then top with cheese and serve.

Per Serving Count	
Carbohydrate	3
Protein	8
Fat	2

Tofu and Vegetable Stir Fry

(4 servings)

1 Tbsp. olive oil
1 package extra-firm or firm tofu, cubed
2 cups broccoli
1 bag shredded angel hair cabbage
1 bag cleaned and washed spinach leaves
1 large zucchini
1 large onion
6 cloves garlic
1 can black beans, rinsed and drained

Sauté onion and garlic in olive oil. Add tofu and continue to sauté on low heat. Cover and let simmer for five minutes. Add cabbage, zucchini, broccoli and spinach. Allow to cook and incorporate flavors. Then add can of black beans and simmer for another 5-10 minutes.

Per Serving Count	
Carbohydrate	1
Protein	2
Fat	1

Vegetable Chow Mein

(serves 6)

1-2 tsp. olive oil
3 large onions, sliced
4 cups sliced celery
1 pound mushrooms, chopped
1 can bamboo shoots
1 can water chestnuts
1 cup bean sprouts
3 ½ cups water
¼ light soy sauce
Pepper to taste
¼ cup cornstarch
¼ cup water

In a large saucepan, heat oil and sauté onions until lightly brown. Add celery, mushrooms, bean sprouts, bamboo shoots, water chestnuts, 3 ½ cups water, and ¼ cup light soy sauce. Season to taste with pepper. Simmer for 15-20 minutes or until vegetables are tender. Combine cornstarch and 1/4 cup water. Stir into vegetable mixture and continue to cook, stirring until thickened. Optional: serve over brown rice. Add cooked shrimp or poultry to have a complete meal.

Per Serving Count	
Carbohydrate	2
Protein	0
Fat	1

Vegetable Cutlets

(serves 8)

6 medium potatoes
¼ cup olive oil
2 onions, chopped
6 mushrooms, chopped
2-3 chopped carrots
1 bunch broccoli, chopped
1 cup corn
1 cup chopped zucchini
3 egg whites
2 cups bread crumbs
Salt and pepper to taste

Preheat oven to 350 degrees. Cook potatoes in boiling water 20 minutes or until tender. Peel and mash. In a skillet, sauté the onions and mushrooms until tender. Pour onion/mushroom mixture into bowl with mashed potatoes. Stir in the rest of the vegetables with the eggs. Mix thoroughly. Add enough bread crumbs so that the mixture can be made into patties. Season with salt and pepper. Shape into about 10 patties. Spray Pam on cookie sheet and bake for about 45 minutes or until slightly browned.

Per Serving Count	
Carbohydrate	3
Protein	0
Fat	1

Veggie Mexican

(serves 4)

1 Tbsp. olive oil
½ cup chopped onions
½ cup chopped mushrooms
1 15-ounce can of red kidney beans, drained and rinsed very well
1 ¾ cup low-sodium/fat-free chicken broth
10 ounce frozen corn
1 cup chunky salsa
½ cup brown rice dry
¼ cup dry lentils, rinsed
1-cup broccoli and zucchini, diced
½ tsp. chili powder
½ tsp. garlic powder

Brown onions in olive oil and then add everything in order. You may want to add other vegetables or grains. If you add grains, add the appropriate amount of water. Let this mixture simmer for 20-30 minutes or until rice is tender. Can be served in a tortilla and/or with salad.

Per Serving Count	
Carbohydrate	3
Protein	2
Fat	1

Vegetarian Stuffed Cabbage

(serves 4)

1 large head green cabbage
1 cup brown rice, cooked
1 carrot
1 green pepper
2 stalks celery
1 broccoli
1 onion
6 mushrooms
Salt and pepper
2-3 tsp. olive oil
1 large jar of tomato sauce

Core cabbage. Cover with water and boil hard for 30 minutes. Remove 18 leaves from cabbage and shred 2 cups of remaining cabbage. Cook rice until tender. Preheat oven to 350 degrees. Grind or finely chop broccoli, carrot, green pepper, celery, onion and mushrooms. Sauté in 2-3 tsp. olive oil until mushy but not brown. Stir vegetables into rice. Stir in salt and pepper to taste. Place one heaping Tbsp. on each cabbage leaf. Fold over leaf filling once, turn in sides of leaf and continue rolling. Line pan with tomato sauce and cover cabbage with sauce. Cover with foil and bake for 1 ½ hours on 350 degrees.

Per Serving Count	
Carbohydrate	3
Protein	0
Fat	1

Desserts

Applesauce-Oatmeal Cookies

(2 dozen)

3 cups oatmeal
1 cup whole-wheat flour
1 tsp. baking soda
¼ tsp. nutmeg
1 cup unsweetened applesauce
½ cup sugar
1 tsp. vanilla
2/3 cup raisins, cranberries, or dried apples
½ cup chopped walnuts

Combine the first four ingredients. Mix up the next three ingredients and add them to the dry ingredients. Stir in the dried fruit and nuts. Roll in small balls and smash to ¼ inch thickness on the cookie sheet. Bake at 275 degrees for 20-25 minutes.

Per Serving Count	
Carbohydrate	2
Protein	0
Fat	1

Fat-Free Yogurt Dessert

(serves 1)

½ cup fat-free vanilla yogurt
1 cup berries
1 Tbsp. flaxseed meal, unprocessed bran or wheat germ
¾ cup Kashi's *Good Friends* Cereal
1 Tbsp. chocolate sprinkles

This makes a very high-fiber nutritious snack.

Per Serving Count	
Carbohydrate	3
Protein	0
Fat	0

Fresh Fruit Compote

(serves 4)

Seedless red grapes (large bunch)
Medium pineapple (chunked)
2 tart apples
Dozen cherries (pitted and halved)
1 cup of blueberries, raspberries and/or strawberries
¼ cup brandy or liqueur of choice

Combine all ingredients in a clear glass bowl with ¼ cup brandy to moisten all the fruit well. Let marinate in refrigerator for a few hours before serving. Serve with a dollop of *Stonyfield Farms* Fat-Free French Vanilla Yogurt or Sorbet.

Per Serving Count	
Carbohydrate	3
Protein	0
Fat	0

Fruit Crepe Dessert

(serves 1)

Microwave crepe for 15-20 seconds (buy at local supermarket in produce section with berries)
Add berries of your choice and banana slices
Add some light whipped cream or *Cool Whip* and serve.
Add 4 walnuts, chopped

Per Serving Count	
Carbohydrate	1
Protein	0
Fat	2

Rice Pudding

(12 servings)

4 eggs, 8 egg whites, or 1 cup egg substitute
¾ cup sugar
2 cups skim plus milk
1 Tbsp. vanilla extract
1 Tbsp. cinnamon
3 cups cooked long-grain brown rice

Preheat oven to 325 degrees. Spray a baking dish with *Pam.* Mix eggs and sugar well together in a bowl. Add the milk, flavoring and again mix well. Then add the cooked rice and mix, while making sure it is evenly distributed in bowl. Pour into baking dish and bake for 40-45 minutes or until the center is set and beginning to pull away from the sides of the dish. Serve cooled.

Per Serving Count	
Carbohydrate	2
Protein	0
Fat	0

Trail Mix Snack

(serves 1)

3/4 cup Kashi's *Good Friends* cereal
4 chopped walnuts
6 slivered almonds
¼ cup dried blueberries or apricots

Mix together and enjoy!

Per Serving Count	
Carbohydrate	2
Protein	0
Fat	3

Chapter Five: Staying Healthy

The Diet Game

by Randy Gossman

Marci Page Sloane MS, RD, LD/N, CDE

Attention-Deficit/Hyperactivity Disorder

Millions of American children and approximately 3% of the adult population have been diagnosed with Attention-Deficit/Hyperactivity Disorder or ADHD. The main symptoms are reduced attentiveness and concentration, hyperactivity, distractibility and impulsiveness. Recently, researchers found subtle differences in the brain structure and metabolism between children with and without ADHD.

Can diet trigger worsening symptoms?

Methylphenidate, more commonly known as Ritalin, is a frequently prescribed drug for this condition. Some reported side effects of Ritalin and other drugs such as Adderall, an amphetamine, used to treat ADHD are reduced appetite and weight loss, stomachaches and insomnia. Furthermore, long-term studies have not been done to determine the effects of these drugs later in life. A study done by the National Toxicology Program found moderate doses of Ritalin to cause liver cancer in mice. Although medications are sometimes required to control the symptoms parents might want to consider other measures first.

Many children who have sensitivities to foods or allergies may have worsening symptoms from particular foods they consume. In a majority of studies done to determine the effect of food dyes, artificial flavors, monosodium glutamate, some food preservatives, and common food allergens such as milk, wheat, eggs and chocolate, children were shown to have increased symptoms. It appears that a child with ADHD who has food allergies or sensitivities may be helped by dietary changes. Eliminating possible food allergens would be the first step in determining if your child could improve without the use of drugs.

Just think of how many foods contain dyes, preservatives, artificial flavorings, artificial sweeteners and other additives. Foods like candy, beverages, cakes, desserts, sweetened cereals, and many other foods frequently consumed by children. Studies were also done to determine if the reason for worsening symptoms was simply from eating high-sugar foods. This was not found to be the case, however, in the majority of children tested. When people have food allergies, you must eliminate all questionable foods and then re-introduce them one at a time in order to determine which foods may be responsible for allergic reactions. Similarly, ADHD symptoms may be enhanced in those with food sensitivities. Children with asthma, hives, hay fever or other allergy-type conditions are the most likely to benefit from dietary changes.

The first step would be to address the food issue. Eliminate certain possible trigger foods and pay attention to your child's behavior. If no difference is noted then behavioral counseling and possibly medication would be warranted. Update: Promising studies are currently being done to determine the effects of omega 3 fats on children with mental health issues.

Beverages

Water is the best choice of beverage for the day. Water is a non-caloric beverage that is required for life! It helps protect the body from dehydration and allows for the body to function most efficiently. Consuming many foods, including fruits and vegetables, is another way to increase your water intake as well as drinking herbal teas, club soda, or juices.

Fruit juice is a healthy way to consume water and nutrients together. However, there are approximately 150 calories in each eight-ounce glass and 30 grams of carbohydrates.

Vegetable juice is another healthy way to consume water and nutrients together. There are approximately 50 calories in each eight-ounce glass and only 11 grams of carbohydrates. Please use only the lower-sodium versions.

Coffee is a very popular beverage in the United States. It is safe to drink and quite enjoyable to most of us. Please consume this drink in moderation, though, as it contains high levels of caffeine that will dehydrate you. If you have hypertension, heart problems or other health issues you may be concerned about, try decaffeinated coffee or discuss the effects of drinking this beverage with your doctor.

Tea is gaining popularity in this country. Green, black and white tea all contain compounds that offer antioxidant properties. If you are prone to kidney stones (calcium oxalate stones) please refrain from drinking tea since it is rich in oxalates.

Milk should be consumed in moderation. It contains fat, calories, and sugar. If the milk is not organic or does not indicate that its manufacturers are opposed to the use of Bovine Growth Hormone (a hormone that is injected into cows for more efficient production of milk) it may also increase your risk of certain gynecological cancers. Each eight-ounce glass of milk has 12 grams of carbohydrates and an ounce of protein.

Soda is a high-caloric beverage that is primarily water and sugar. Dark sodas like root beer and cola contain higher levels of phosphorous and therefore encourage your body to leach calcium from the bones. I do not recommend these drinks.

Diet soda is a non-caloric beverage that is primarily water and chemicals. Please limit your consumption of this beverage. If it contains caffeine it is also dehydrating and will not count as water. In fact you will need extra water. I do not recommend this drink.

Alcoholic beverages used in moderation, which is to say one drink a day for women and two drinks a day for men, can be heart protective. You must check with your doctor and/or pharmacist to make sure alcohol is safe for you and does not interact with any medications that you may be taking.

People with diabetes must be careful when drinking alcohol since it can result in low blood sugar. Think about it: after drinking alcohol, don't you feel hungry? This is because alcohol inhibits the liver from regulating your blood sugar. In other words, your liver stores sugar and when your blood sugar drops, ordinarily, the liver will send out its stored sugar into the bloodstream to lift your blood sugar back up to normal levels. However, when you drink alcohol, the liver's primary job is to get rid of this toxin! It focuses on filtering out the alcohol before it raises your blood sugar level to normal. A small carbohydrate snack will help you to maintain normal blood sugar levels. Please account for the additional calories for your alcoholic drinks. On average, an alcoholic drink is between 100 and 150 calories. This is for six ounces of wine, twelve ounces of beer or two ounces of liquor. The proof of the alcohol in an ounce of the drink must be multiplied by two. Wine is 12.5% alcohol so it is said to be 25-proof. Beer is approximately 6% alcohol so it is 12-proof. Liquor is typically 80-proof. The exact formula is: alcoholic calories = 0.8 x proof of the drink x number of ounces consumed. Take a six-ounce glass of wine as an example:0.8 x proof (25) x ounces (6) = 120 calories.

Bone Health

Foods to Maintain Strong Bones:

♦ Calcium works in conjunction with magnesium and vitamin D. Foods with high calcium levels are milk, (try Parmalat skim milk plus) yogurt, cheese, spinach, kale, broccoli, collard greens, beans, figs, tofu, sardines, seaweed, almonds and calcium-fortified orange juice.

♦ Magnesium, in addition to calcium and vitamin D, works to maintain strong bones. Foods with high magnesium levels are almonds, bananas, beans, cashews, flounder, milk, miso, oatmeal, peanuts, potatoes, spinach, tofu, wheat germ, and yogurt.

♦ Vitamin D is critical to help your body use calcium. Foods high in vitamin D include eel, sardines, herring, salmon, tuna, and milk. Your body absorbs enough vitamin D from the sun if you're under 60 years of age.

Foods that May Harm Bones:
♦ Excessive caffeine reduces calcium levels in the body. Drink fewer than three cups of coffee a day.
♦ Excessive sodium reduces calcium levels in the body. Keep your intake at less than 3,000 mg/day.
♦ Excessive protein reduces calcium levels in the body. This is one danger of high-protein diets.
♦ Ask your doctor about an osteoporosis screening test using the DEXA (dual energy x-ray absorptiometry).

Cancer

One-third of all cancers are diet-related. Foods can help a person cleanse the body and keep the immune system and the body strong. Wholesome foods like whole grains, fruits, vegetables and legumes can accomplish this. Foods laden with chemicals, artificial sweeteners, like fat-free or sugar-free foods, offer the body an unnatural environment that may encourage disease.

Foods to help prevent cancer include:
♦ Cruciferous vegetables like cabbage, broccoli, collard or mustard greens, Brussels sprouts
♦ Allium vegetables like onions, garlic, leeks
♦ Lycopene foods like tomatoes and apricots
♦ Green tea, black tea and white tea
♦ Fiber foods like oats, beans, and bran
♦ Monounsaturated fats like olive oil, nuts, avocado
♦ Omega-3 fats like salmon, flaxseed (use same precautions as soy), walnuts

♦ Beta carotene foods like apricots, peaches, sweet potatoes, carrots, collard greens, spinach (both dark leafy green and orange fruits and vegetables)
♦ Mushrooms like shitake and maitake
♦ Vegetarian diet including soy (those at high risk for breast cancer should consume soy products three times per week) and many wholesome foods.
♦ Resveratrol containing foods like blueberries, red grapes and peanuts
♦ Avoid foods that clog up the body. High-fat foods, processed and convenience foods, trans fats or partially hydrogenated fats, poor quality foods found in fast food restaurants, cold cuts, bacon, bologna or salami containing nitrates, cured or smoked meats, or animal foods containing hormones
♦ Spices such as turmeric, parsley or rosemary
♦ Brazil nuts containing selenium
♦ Relax, laugh, meditate and be positive!

Cholesterol

What is cholesterol?
Cholesterol is a white, waxy substance made by the liver that is *only found in animal products.*

Is all cholesterol bad?
HDL or high-density lipoproteins are good for the heart. If above 50 mg/dL, they protect the heart by helping to clear plaque out of your arteries.

LDL or low-density lipoproteins are very bad for the heart. They should be under 130 mg/dL, or under 100 mg/dL if you are taking cholesterol-lowering medications. LDLs build artery-clogging plaque. You want to avoid consuming trans fats, saturated fats and too many sweets. Trans fat and saturated fat both encourage the liver to produce extra cholesterol and a more dangerous form than the cholesterol found in foods. They are the *culprit* in heart disease.

Do I need a breakdown of cholesterol, or is the total enough information?
Total cholesterol does not give you enough information. You must know how high the HDLs are and how low the LDLs are.

How can I lower my LDL (lousy) cholesterol?
♦ Low saturated-fat, trans fat and cholesterol meal plan
♦ Lose weight if you need to
♦ Increase monounsaturated fats
♦ Increase soluble fiber
♦ Increase omega-3 fats

How can I increase my HDL (healthy) cholesterol?
♦ Aerobic exercise such as walking, swimming, bicycling five times a week for 45 minutes with the approval of your physician
♦ Weight loss if needed
♦ Soy products (tofu, soy milk, soy cheese, edamame)
♦ Garlic (roasted tastes great!)
♦ Foods containing the antioxidant resveratrol such as blueberries, red wine, red grapes and peanuts
♦ Moderate alcohol intake (if approved by your doctor): one drink per day for women and two drinks per day for men

Cholesterol/saturated fat amounts in protein

Food Category	Food (3 ounces)	Saturated Fat (grams)	Cholesterol (mg)
Shellfish	Lobster	.1	61
	Shrimp	.2	166
	Sea Scallops	.6	34
Fish	Snapper	.3	40
	Flounder/Sole	.3	58
	Sea Bass	.6	45
	Salmon	1	42
	Swordfish	1.2	43
	Tuna, canned	1	35
Poultry	Chicken, white	1	73
	Chicken, dark	3	80
	Turkey, white	.2	71
	Turkey, dark	1	101
Pork	Bacon	15	72
	Ham	3	50
	Loin	3	83
	Sausage	9	69
	Spareribs	10	103
Beef	Frankfurter	11	54
	Ground Beef	6	83
	Liver	2	331
	Lunch meats	10	54
	T-bone steak	9	71
	Tenderloin	4	73
	Top Round	2	72

According to the Environmental Protection Agency (EPA) fish high in mercury levels to avoid are swordfish, shark, tilefish, and king mackerel. Canned albacore (white) tuna should only be consumed three times a week. Safer, lower mercury fish are shellfish, and smaller ocean fish. A January 2004 study showed the amount of PCBs (polychlorinated biphenyls) and other potentially cancer-causing contaminants in farm-raised (Atlantic) salmon exceeds the amount found in wild Pacific or Alaskan (Pink or Sockeye) salmon. Until fish farmers choose healthier fish-feed please consume Atlantic salmon once a month. Stay tuned for further developments.

Chronic Obstructive Pulmonary Disease

Chronic Obstructive Pulmonary Disease (COPD) is a respiratory disease. Emphysema and chronic bronchitis are two respiratory diseases with which you are probably already familiar. Respiration is the complete cycle of breathing in and out. When you breathe in (inhale), oxygen enters the lungs. When you breathe out (exhale), carbon dioxide leaves the lungs and the body.

When a person has COPD, less oxygen enters the lungs upon inhalation, and not all of the carbon dioxide leaves the lungs and the body upon exhalation.

Since a person with COPD is not releasing all of the carbon dioxide, it is important to consume foods that produce the least amount of carbon dioxide. Carbohydrates (starch, fruit, milk, sweets) produce the highest amount of carbon dioxide. With less carbon dioxide in the body, you will be able to breathe more easily.

Eating for COPD:

♦ When consuming carbohydrates, be sure to make healthy choices. Consume higher fiber carbohydrates from whole grains, fruits, and vegetables. Do not consume large amounts of these at any given meal, since they produce more carbon dioxide and will make it more difficult for you to breathe.

♦ Consume protein (fish, poultry, lean meat) in order for your respiratory muscles to stay strong.

♦ Healthy fats such as monounsaturated or polyunsaturated may be consumed. These fats add up in calories but they produce the least amount of carbon dioxide.

♦ Don't overeat sodium-containing foods. Your blood pressure may increase, or swelling in the body may occur. Aim for about 2,000 mg of sodium a day.

♦ Try to consume six small meals a day in order to allow your body to digest these foods without them making you feel bloated and full – making it more difficult for you to breathe.

♦ Eat slowly. By eating quickly you may create more distention in your stomach with excessive air or gas.

Cirrhosis

Cirrhosis is a progressive liver disease that's usually brought on by alcoholism. Still, malaria, syphilis, viral hepatitis, drugs, blocked bile ducts or even malnutrition also can cause the disease. Cirrhosis causes the liver cells to die and be replaced by scar tissue. This scar tissue does not enable the liver to function properly. The liver is responsible for breaking down carbohydrates, protein and fat. It also detoxifies (or filters out) alcohol, drugs and other toxins. The liver stores vitamins B12, A, D, K and iron. It produces cholesterol and bile, which help in digesting fats, in addition to substances that are essential for blood clotting.

For someone in the early stages of cirrhosis, the first step is to eliminate alcohol or other toxins that may be contributing to the disease. Carbohydrates become a major part of the diet and protein relies mainly on vegetable protein like soy products and beans in addition to dairy protein like milk, yogurt, and eggs. If there is swelling sodium is reduced significantly as is fluid.

Symptoms may include: loss of appetite, nausea, vomiting, weight loss, swelling and jaundice

Nutrition:
- Protein foods should be evenly distributed over the day not to overwhelm the liver's functions
- Mostly dairy/vegetable protein should be consumed
- Calorie requirements are increased due to fast metabolism
- Consume lower protein and higher carbohydrates
- Have 25% - 40% of total calories from fat
- Stay away from saturated fat, refined sugar and alcohol
- Increase soluble fibers such as oats, beans, apples and barley for natural cleansing

- ◆ Cruciferous vegetables such as cabbage, broccoli, and Brussels sprouts as well as sulfur-containing foods like garlic, onions and eggs also aid in liver function
- ◆ With severe swelling, reduce fluid/sodium (your physician may prescribe 1,000 – 1,500 cc or 4-6 cups of fluid per day and 1,000 mg sodium)
- ◆ Vitamin supplementation with B-complex, K, calcium, zinc, and magnesium are given due to the liver's poor absorption of these vitamins. Copper and manganese should NOT be recommended since they cannot be excreted. Often a multivitamin will be recommended in addition.
- ◆ Ask your doctor about using Milk Thistle. This plant-based, over-the-counter herb has been shown to protect the liver against further damage and enhances its detoxifying abilities. Be sure that it contains at least 80% of the anti-oxidant compound, silymarin.

Constipation

Constipation is a common problem for people who consume the typical American diet, which includes processed and refined foods, few whole grains, fruits or vegetables (low fiber), high sodium, and soda or coffee. To avoid the discomfort and frustration of constipation, you simply need to increase water consumption to at least eight 8-ounce glasses a day, increase fiber to at least 30 grams a day, and eat fruits and vegetables (both of which contain fiber and water). Exercise also helps your bowels to move more efficiently. Being sedentary adds to the problem of constipation. Start increasing insoluble fiber like bran and wheat products. You can consume *Wheatena*, for example, and add two Tbsp. of unprocessed bran. Then drink eight ounces of prune juice or eat five or six stewed prunes. Walk briskly at least fifteen to thirty minutes a day. You should notice changes in your bowel movements if you follow this regimen. You can also try making a trail mix to use as a daily snack that includes a high fiber, whole wheat cereal like Kashi's *Good Friends* or *Shredded Wheat n' Bran* and mix it with dried figs, prunes, or dates. High-sodium foods and excessive coffee, tea or soda (with caffeine) will dehydrate you and add to your already existing problems! Fiber needs water in order to move through your digestive system. Therefore, it's really important for you to drink water, especially if you add fiber foods. If you take *Metamucil* (psyllium) or other aids, please drink enough fluids to help them work as well!

Coumadin

There are many misconceptions about what to do when a person needs to take this drug. Coumadin is a blood-thinner. It's not the only blood-thinner that you can take: garlic, vitamin E, Ginkgo Biloba, aspirin and fish oil are just a few others. The main concern of many people on Coumadin is eating certain vitamin K foods that you love, such as green leafy vegetables like salads, spinach or broccoli. Vitamin K is a coagulant (it helps the blood to clot) and Coumadin is an anti-coagulant (it helps to thin the blood to reduce clotting). In other words, the more vitamin K you eat, the less the Coumadin will work, and the more Coumadin you may need to take.

Another potential problem with Coumadin is the amount of blood thinners you are taking that you don't realize. Don't freely self-medicate with herbs if you don't know anything about them. How many people know, for example, that Gingko Biloba mixed with Coumadin or aspirin can cause a hemorrhagic stroke due to the abundance of blood-thinning agents in all of these medications?

The most important thing for you to do is to stay consistent and not be excessive. When your Coumadin levels were set, you were eating certain vitamin K foods already. If you suddenly stop eating these foods, then you may need less Coumadin. If you continue eating as you usually do, then your Coumadin probably won't need to be changed very often. The problem is that these vitamin K foods are very healthy and you shouldn't avoid them. If you are on a high dose of Coumadin, you need to be more careful, and keep a stricter eye than usual on your diet.

Latest news: Soy products, like tofu, and soymilk, contain substances called genistein and daidzein that may interfere with the body's absorption of Coumadin. In other words, stay consistent and don't overeat soy products if you are on Coumadin! Similarly, Coenzyme Q10 (CoQ10) may reduce the effectiveness of Coumadin.

Diabetes Mellitus

Diabetes is the inability of the body to process or metabolize foods efficiently. This is due to either a lack or inefficient use of insulin.

Insulin is a hormone responsible for aiding in metabolism by converting food into energy. Insulin carries the sugar out of the bloodstream and into the body's cells (such as the brain, tissues, and muscles). You have millions of cells that have to be fed with sugar (glucose) or you can't survive. This works in a way similar to how a car's gas tank works. A car must be fed with fuel to function – and so must you!

In Type 1 diabetes, the pancreas makes no insulin. In order for the person to survive, he or she must take insulin injections. Without insulin he/she can starve to death. "Starvation in the midst of plenty", quoted by William Castle, refers to a person with Type 1 diabetes who produces no insulin to feed the body's cells with sugar (fuel). Although they are eating "plenty" of food (sugar or fuel), the lack of insulin would result in "starvation". In Type 2 diabetes, also known as insulin resistance, (the insulin resists working), the person's insulin is "lazy" and doesn't work hard enough to move the sugar out of the bloodstream and into the cells. Therefore, the blood sugar goes higher than normal. This excessive blood sugar can lead to many diseases of the vessels: retinopathy or damage to the eye vessels, nephropathy or damage to the kidney's vessels, neuropathy or damage to the nerve vessels, heart disease or damage to the vessels leading to and from the heart, and circulation problems leading to amputation. Both exercise and weight loss (if necessary) can decrease insulin resistance. Blood sugar will improve with a weight loss of ten pounds.

The good news is that diabetes is a very controllable disease; it is a disease that can be self-managed. This means that each person with diabetes has the choice of controlling his or her own disease. Most of this control is done through meal planning. Sometimes people with Type 2 diabetes also need pills and/or insulin to control their diabetes. However, food choices must be considered, no matter what the medication regimen or type of diabetes.

Carbohydrates are foods that have the greatest impact on blood sugar. This is because they turn 100% into sugar within one to two hours after eating them.

Carbohydrates include foods such as starches, vegetables, legumes, fruits, milks and sweets. Protein (meat, fish, poultry, eggs and cheese) turns 50% into sugar, but it takes hours to do so. These foods do not have a major impact on your blood sugar. If you overeat them, however, you may put extra stress on the heart and the kidneys. Fat (oils, sauces, and butters) turn only 10% into sugar. These foods do not increase your blood sugar level.

Main guidelines to follow:
For Type 1 diabetes, meal planning and insulin are used together for tight control of blood sugar. For Type 2 diabetes, you have to make insulin's job easier!
1. Limit carbohydrates at each meal or snack.
2. Evenly distribute carbohydrates throughout the day (see food serving size list).
3. Consume slow-digesting foods or food combinations in order for your "lazy" insulin to have an easier job. These foods include:
   a. High-fiber carbohydrates (35-50 grams a day of fiber)
   b. Combining lean protein and carbohydrates
   c. Combining unsaturated fat and carbohydrates

4. Consume approximately 30-45 grams of total carbohydrate per meal (depending on your calories for the day and how your glucose is running).
5. Consume approximately 15–30 grams of total carbohydrate per snack.
6. Test your blood sugar before meals and after meals to determine if your body can handle the amount of carbohydrates you've eaten. If not, decrease the amount of carbohydrates or you may need a medication adjustment.
7. Look for the following results when testing blood sugar:
   ♦ Before meals blood sugar should be 80-120 mg/dL
   ♦ 1 ½ hours after finishing a meal blood sugar should be under 140 mg/dL (at most, 160!)
   ♦ Blood sugar can expect to rise about 50 points from a meal.
   ♦ If your blood sugar reading is 150 mg/dL before your meal and 200 mg/dL 1 ½ hours after eating, that means your body was able to process the sugar from that meal very well. Your blood sugar simply started higher than it should have.
8. Eat every 4-5 hours so your blood sugar doesn't drop or fluctuate too much. This may determine whether a snack is necessary or not.
9. Wait 2 hours between meals and snacks so the blood sugar has a chance to come down before you send it up with the next food consumption.
10. Have your doctor do a blood test to determine your 3-month blood sugar average. HbA1c, also known as glycohemoglobin or hemoglobin A1c, shows the progress you are making every few months with controlling your diabetes. Look for a number of 6% for

good control. This means you are running 120 mg/dL on average over 3 months. Fructosamine is a similar test that averages two weeks worth of blood sugar results.

11. By delaying digestion, you will slow down the release of sugar into the bloodstream, thereby making insulin's job of getting the sugar out of the bloodstream and into the cells a lot easier. The way to slow down the release of sugar into the bloodstream is to slow down its digestion.

12. When looking at food labels, be sure to look at total carbohydrate, NOT SUGAR, when trying to determine how high in sugar a food is. The sugar listed is included in the total carbohydrate. It refers to refined sugar, like fruit sugar, milk sugar or table sugar. The total carbohydrate encompasses everything in that food that will eventually become sugar. Dietary fiber may, however, be subtracted from the total carbohydrate, since fiber is a non-digestible part of the carbohydrate.

Did you know? Cinnamon may improve blood sugar levels by consuming ¼ teapsoon per day.

Gestational Diabetes

Estrogen, cortisol, and other hormones produced by the placenta begin to block the effects of insulin during pregnancy. If the pancreas cannot produce enough additional insulin to overcome the effects of the hormones, diabetes during pregnancy results.

<u>Goal Blood Glucose Levels</u>
Fasting: 60-90 mg/dL

Before meals: 60-105 mg/dL
1 hour after meals: Under 140 mg/dL
2 hours after meals: Under 120 mg/dL

Patients are usually asked to test their blood glucose levels fasting, and again two hours after the start of each meal. It is critical that these blood sugars are in the range listed above. Notify your doctor and/or dietitian/nurse educator if these numbers are higher.

Nutrition:
Avoid simple carbohydrates such as fruit juice, cakes and candy unless you test your blood glucose before and two hours from the start of the meal or snack and your results fall in the safe range. Evenly distribute your carbohydrates (starch, fruit and milk) during meals and snacks. Do not drink more than one eight-ounce glass of milk at one time. Do not have milk or fruit at breakfast when your blood sugar tends to run higher (unless your blood sugar is in excellent control and your body can handle it). Have no more than 30 grams of carbohydrates for breakfast. Do not use saccharin (*Sweet 'n Low*) because it crosses through the placenta. Aspartame (*Equal/NutraSweet)* and sucralose (Splenda) can be used moderately (2-4 servings per day). Make sure to have a snack at night of carbohydrate with protein and/or fat to decrease the chance of having positive ketones in the morning urine.

Light exercise, like walking, is important for your health and to lower your blood sugar. If you are already in an exercise program, you may exercise at higher intensities with the approval of your doctor.

Ketones (a toxic by-product that results from improper fat breakdown) must be checked each morning at your first urination. This is done by placing the ketone strip in the urine. If you have not eaten enough carbohydrates, your body must get its energy from another source. The body then breaks down fat for fuel. If your body is not utilizing the carbohydrates efficiently, high blood sugar results and ketones again are used for fuel by breaking down fat.

♦ If ketones are positive and blood sugar is normal or low, call your dietitian to adjust your diet.

♦ If ketones are positive and blood sugar is high, call your doctor.

♦ If ketones are negative and blood sugar is high, call your dietitian for an adjustment in your diet.

♦ If ketones are negative and blood sugar is normal, you are doing very well and continue what you are doing.

Sugar passes from mother to baby through the placenta. Insulin does not pass from mother to baby. After the 12th week of pregnancy, the baby can make its own insulin. If the mother consistently has high blood sugar, the baby will overproduce insulin. Excess sugar and insulin will cause your baby to gain weight, which will result in an overweight baby.

Keep track of your baby's movement by counting fetal movements or "kicks." After the 26th week of pregnancy when your baby is most active, start "kick counting." After a meal, sit on a comfortable chair and write down how many times your baby moves. You should expect about 10 kicks at a time. If you do not feel your baby kicking, contact your doctor.

Sugar-free Foods

Carbohydrates are foods that turn completely into sugar. They include starch, fruit and milk. Sugar-free foods may not be carbohydrate-free.

Sugar-free foods are simply an unhealthy substitute for low-fat or regular foods. They contain sugar alcohols and other ingredients that turn completely into sugar, which are not listed under sugar on the food label. They are, however, listed under total carbohydrate. People with diabetes often eat these foods freely, not realizing that both sugar alcohol and sugar make blood glucose rise. Sugar alcohols such as mannitol, sorbitol, xylitol and maltitol turn into glucose at varying rates depending on their caloric value. Sugar alcohols have between 1 and 4 calories for each gram while sugar has 4 calories per gram. Lower calorie sugar alcohols will have less of an impact on blood glucose - clearly a benefit to the person with diabetes. However, due to the slower rate of absorption, they produce abdominal cramps, gas and diarrhea. Foods containing sugar alcohol also costs the consumer more. These foods always contain one or more artificial sweeteners. The most disturbing issue is that people with diabetes do not expect these foods to raise their blood sugar. They assume these foods contain no sugar and therefore they can be free to eat as much as they would like. This results in uncontrolled blood sugar. Testing your blood sugar before and 1 1/2 hours after consuming these foods will reveal their impact on you. The alternative is to consume a healthier, wholesome product that includes natural sugar but has no artificial ingredients. Natural foods actually taste a lot better and cost a lot less.

They may also ward off other diseases to which the body is more susceptible. Please be aware of the new low carb foods. Their food labels emphasize *net carbs* which is the total carbohydrate minus the dietary fiber and the sugar alcohols. While dietary fiber has minimal, if any, impact on blood sugar these sugar alcohols will affect it. What is not clear is the individual affect of these sugar alcohols since the ones with fewer calories will have the least impact on a person's blood sugar. Further, low carbohydrate foods take out some carbohydrates and replace them with saturated fat and artificial ingredients. Be careful!

The American Diabetes Association's 2002 Clinical Nutritional Recommendations suggests that there is no evidence that foods containing sugar alcohol result in a significant reduction in calories or blood glucose.

Let's compare a popular sugar-free vanilla wafer cookie to a supermarket brand of vanilla wafers. Many people with diabetes eat sugar-free cookies. They pay more and assume these cookies will have no effect on their blood glucose. The mistake here is that people always correlate diabetes with sugar. People with diabetes rightfully fear possible complications such as heart disease, kidney disease, nerve disease, eye disease and amputation. When they see sugar-free foods they find a new lease on life. Just think how happy the person with diabetes feels when he/she comes across sugar-free chocolate, sugar-free cookies, and no sugar-added ice cream! And think of how frightening it is to find out that one has been misguided into believing these foods were safe for a diabetic, when they clearly are not. In eight sugar-free vanilla wafers, there are

120 calories, 4 grams of total fat and 1 gram of saturated fat, *23 grams of total carbohydrate* and 0 grams of sugar. In eight sugar vanilla wafers, there are 120 calories, 3 grams of total fat, 1 gram of saturated fat, *21 grams of total carbohydrate and 11 grams of sugar.* In addition, the ingredient list on the sugar-free cookies is twice as long as the regular cookie label because there are twice as many additives!

What exactly does this mean? Carbohydrates turn 100% into sugar except for the part containing fiber. Carbohydrates are starch, fruit and milk. This means that any food such as cookies (contains flour or starch), ice cream (contains milk), or food made with fruit (contains fruit) cannot possibly be sugar-free since the carbohydrate part of these foods turns completely into sugar! They may be naturally sugar-free, but they certainly are not carbohydrate-free. What you have to do is read the total carbohydrate on a food label. The sugar, sugar alcohol and any other ingredient that will turn into sugar will and must be listed under total carbohydrate. This cannot deceive you. While the FDA may find artificial sweeteners safe, I question their use. It's better to eat a more natural food if you can. In this case the sugar-free cookies give you more fat and total carbohydrate (sugar) than the real cookies! If you choose to use an artificial sweetener please use Splenda (sucralose) or Stevia in moderation.

In conclusion, sugar alcohol affects your blood glucose and can lead to diabetes complications. It is also contained in lower quality foods. You must look closely at your food labels and at the total carbohydrate to determine what is really affecting your blood glucose.

Diverticulosis

Diverticulosis is a very common condition of the intestine. About half of all Americans aged 60-80 and almost everyone over age 80 has it. When you have diverticulosis, small pouches called diverticula in your colon bulge out. This is mostly due to the American diet of refined carbohydrates and very little fiber and water that results in frequent constipation. From years of constipation and straining during bowel movements a person may develop these pouches that protrude from the intestine wall. When the pouches become infected or inflamed the disease progresses to a more serious form of diverticulitis. You must avoid foods that may get stuck in the pouches like seeds, nuts and skins of some fruits and vegetables. Any food that you feel discomfort from eating should be avoided. Although the latest research states that no foods need to be avoided, if you feel pain in your digestive tract after eating certain foods it would be best to avoid them in the future.

The best treatment for diverticulosis is to consume insoluble fiber foods. Foods with whole wheat and bran are best since they move quickly through your intestine and won't have time to get stuck in the pouches. Be sure to drink plenty of water so the fiber can move through your digestive tract. The insoluble fiber also will help you to avoid recurring constipation.

Esophageal Reflux (GERD)

Esophageal Reflux refers to the regurgitation of stomach acids into the esophagus. The most common symptom is heartburn. Esophageal reflux is usually a mild condition that can be managed medically or nutritionally. In chronic cases, however, it may lead to esophagitis, ulceration, or hemorrhage.

The esophagus is usually protected from reflux of stomach contents by the contraction of the LES, or lower esophageal sphincter. If the LES becomes stretched and weakened it no longer is able to efficiently protect the patient from reflux (regurgitation of stomach acids).

When the LES muscle loosens, it allows the stomach acids to move back into the esophagus, instead of doing its job and holding the stomach acids in the stomach. The feeling of heartburn comes from those stomach acids being in the wrong place!

Nutritional Changes:
♦ Achieve and maintain desirable body weight.
♦ Avoid large meals. If extra calories are needed, have mid-morning and mid-afternoon snacks. Small meals are preferable, since they digest more efficiently and will lessen the chance of reflux.
♦ Avoid eating meals or snacks for at least two hours before lying down. If you must eat late, prop yourself up with a few pillows before lying down.
♦ Take chewable digestive or papaya enzymes with each meal to help with your digestion.

Avoid or limit foods and beverages that relax the LES:
♦ Alcohol
♦ Peppermint or spearmint
♦ Garlic or onion
♦ Chocolate
♦ High-fat foods: fried foods, meats, cream sauces, gravies, margarine or butter, cream, oil, and high-fat salad dressings

Avoid or limit foods and beverages that can be irritating:
♦ Carbonated beverages
♦ Citrus fruit and juices
♦ Coffee (regular or decaf)
♦ Spices
♦ Tomato products
♦ Very hot or very cold foods

Increase foods that do not affect the LES:
♦ Low-fat protein foods (low-fat dairy products, lean meat, chicken, fish)
♦ Carbohydrate foods with a low-fat content (breads, cereals, crackers, fruit, noodles, potatoes, rice and vegetables prepared without added fat)
♦ Drink liquids between meals instead of with meals
♦ Wear loose fitting clothes, especially after meals
♦ Avoid or quit smoking

Fat

All fat contains monounsaturated fat, polyunsaturated fat, and saturated fat in varying amounts.

Monounsaturated fat
These fats raise HDL (healthy cholesterol) and lower LDL (lousy cholesterol). They are highest in olive oil, canola oil, olives, avocado, most nuts, and sesame seeds.

Polyunsaturated fat
These fats lower both HDL and LDL cholesterol. They are not as beneficial as monounsaturated fat. They are highest in soybean oil, corn oil, safflower oil, sunflower oil, and most processed foods.

Trans fat
These fats raise LDLs and lower HDLs and may also be carcinogenic. This is not beneficial to the body! Trans fats are created by partially hydrogenating liquid oils (usually polyunsaturated oils). Years ago, food manufacturers found a process of hardening vegetable oils and creating foods with a longer shelf-life that contained no saturated fat. Unfortunately, in the late 1990s, it was discovered that trans fat was as bad as saturated fat – if not worse. If you see partially hydrogenated oil in the ingredient list of some processed foods, then they contain trans fat.

Saturated fat
These fats work as trans fats do to raise LDLs and lower HDLs. They are found in most animal products: meat, cheese, cream sauces, butter, poultry and some in fish.

They clog your arteries and encourage the liver to produce extra cholesterol in the body. The cholesterol your body produces is more detrimental to your heart's health than the cholesterol found in foods.

Fiber

Fiber is the portion of carbohydrates that does not get digested. It passes almost intact through the digestive tract and is expelled with bowel movements. Without adequate fiber and water, the digestive process will work inefficiently.

There are two types of fiber, water-soluble and water-insoluble. Foods with fiber contain both of these types but in varying amounts.

*Water-**soluble** fiber* forms a gel when it mixes with fluids and moves very slowly through your digestive system. This slow action is great for controlling the appetite, since it forms bulk in the stomach, making one feel full more quickly. It is found in abundance in oats, legumes, barley and fruits. It is good for lowering cholesterol and for slowing down the rise in blood sugar in people with diabetes.

*Water-**insoluble** fiber* does not dissolve but holds onto fluid so it moves more quickly through the digestive system. It is found mainly in bran, wheat and vegetables. It is good for relieving constipation and recurring diverticulosis due to its quick movement.

Remember to drink water, or the fiber will not move successfully through your digestive system!

It is critical to consume between 30 and 50 grams of fiber a day. Fiber carries out many toxins that accumulate in the body and allows the digestive system to work more adequately. Many digestive problems and diseases stem from inadequate fiber intake. People tend to consume refined carbohydrates that are processed and so are lacking in fiber and other nutrients.

Flatulence

Flatulence (also known as "gas") is something we all release several times a day. Most of this gas comes from the fermentation of indigestible carbohydrates by bacteria living in the colon. If we do not digest certain foods, they sit in the colon and ferment over time. The bacteria in the colon encourage the formation of flatulence (hydrogen, methane, carbon dioxide and nitrogen). Gas is usually odorless, however, certain foods may encourage a more offensive odor.

♦ Sulfur-containing foods create such an odor. These are garlic, cabbage, Brussels sprouts, some fruit, caffeinated beverages, beer or chips.

♦ Foods that create the odorless gas are beans, onions, broccoli, cauliflower, apples, bananas, prunes, peas, apricots, and bran products.

♦ Slow-to-digest foods (high-fat foods) have the opportunity to sit in the colon for a longer period of time and may produce more flatulence.

Treatments:

♦ Increase exercise in order to digest your foods more efficiently and decrease the amount of gas.

♦ Use digestive or papaya enzymes to help your digestive process.

♦ *Beano* (an enzyme used to digest some carbohydrates) may also be used. You can find it in health food stores and in drug store chains.

♦ Activated charcoal pills can help to absorb irritants that are causing the flatulence. Be careful not to take them at the same time as other medications.

♦ Be aware of any allergies to milk sugar (lactose). If you tend to have more gas after consuming milk products (milk, cheese, ice cream) then you may be lactose-intolerant. If so, you may use lactose-free milk or take the enzyme you are lacking called lactase.

♦ Eat slowly, and do not use straws or chew gum; they encourage the formation of gas.

♦ Try Pepto-Bismol. It absorbs sulfur in foods and works to decrease flatulence. Check with your doctor if you are taking blood thinners. Pepto-Bismol contains aspirin so you may not be able to use it very often.

♦ Avoid foods with sugar alcohols (sorbitol, xylitol, or mannitol), as well as *Olestra,* a non-absorbable fake fat. They will all encourage gas.

Gluten-Restricted Diet

(for Celiac Disease/Tropical Sprue)

Gluten is a protein found in wheat, rye, oats, buckwheat, barley, and by-products such as malt. (Some people are not sensitive to oats) It may be hidden in many food products that contain grains such as baked goods, desserts, salad dressings, cereals, and other prepared foods.

Gluten intake is restricted for people who are sensitive and unable to digest these grains and by-products; eating them will create stomach problems. In addition, sensitivity to gluten decreases absorption of vitamins and minerals and other nutrients.

Try to consume mostly wholesome foods so you do not mistakenly eat a food with hidden gluten in it.

Foods to Consume:
♦ Protein (lean meat, poultry, fish, eggs, cheese) without sauces or gravies
♦ All vegetables except those creamed with flour
♦ Fresh fruits; canned, dried or fruit juices

- Milk: whole, skim, 1%, 2% or buttermilk.
- Bread made from arrowroot, rice, corn, soybean, potato and gluten-free wheat flour. Be careful that corn bread doesn't contain any wheat or white flour. Cornmeal, rice, and grits may be used.
- All beverages, unless they contain wheat flour
- Sherbet, ice cream (without gluten stabilizers), homemade rice pudding or tapioca pudding, ices
- Salt, pepper, herbs, cornstarch, vinegar, nuts, coconut, dry mustard, gravies made with cornstarch, potato, rice flour or tapioca
- Soups are fine except when thickened with wheat flour. Use cornstarch or potato flour instead.
- Sugar, molasses, jelly or jam, honey, corn syrup

Foods to Avoid:
- Chocolate milk (with cereal additives), malted milk
- All bread and bread products, including bread crumbs, crackers, rolls, bagels, pancakes, waffles, pretzels, matzo (unless the item specifically states that it is gluten-free)
- Cereals with wheat, rye, barley, kasha, oatmeal, buckwheat, pasta, rice, foods fried with breadcrumbs, or breaded foods
- Thickened or prepared fruits
- Salad dressing; some mayonnaise (get the real mayonnaise to be safe!)
- Malted milk products like *Ovaltine*, instant coffees, carbonated beverages with malt, ale, beer, gin, whiskey, vodka
- Ice cream cones, sandwiches, pie

♦ Gravy extracts, mustard, soy sauce, vegetable protein, flour or cereal protein, malt

As you can see, the "foods to avoid" list is very extensive. Be careful, and always read the ingredient list. The longer the ingredient list is, the more you will have to be aware of. Try to consume mostly unprocessed, wholesome foods.

Glycemic Index

The glycemic index is a system in which a number is given to a particular *carbohydrate* food to determine how quickly or slowly the food breaks down into sugar in the bloodstream. This number is important since people tend to consume many high-glycemic index foods - refined carbohydrates (white pasta, white bread, white rice) that turn quickly into glucose (sugar) in our bodies. These foods do not sustain your appetite or energy (blood sugar) level and people end up overeating them.

If you incorporate low-glycemic index foods (foods that turn into sugar slowly), you can sustain a more even energy level and you also will not get hungry very quickly. This is due to non-fluctuating blood sugar. You know that sugar equals energy. When you eat refined or high-glycemic index foods, your blood sugar quickly climbs and then drops. When the blood sugar drops, you feel hungry since your brain signals your body to eat in order to maintain your energy level. However, if you consume mostly low-glycemic index foods, your blood sugar tends to level out and not fluctuate. This results in diminished appetite and a more sustained level of energy! In addition, by metabolizing sugar more slowly and over a longer period of time we have a chance to utilize the sugar or glucose before it gets stored as fat (triglycerides)!

Glycemic Load is a newer and more accurate term. The glycemic index (GI) tells you how rapidly a particular carbohydrate turns into sugar. It does not tell you how much of that carbohydrate in grams is in a serving of food. The Glycemic Load (GL) is the amount of carbohydrate grams in a food multiplied by the GI of that carbohydrate.

You can use the numbers in the charts as a guide. There are many influential variables when dealing with GI or GL. Combinations of food, and how you cook them can change the glycemic index/glycemic load. Since fat, protein, and high-fiber foods digest more slowly, by adding either one to a carbohydrate, the rate of absorption and consequently the glycemic index number will be changed. For example, *Cornflakes* alone have a high glycemic index number. Combining nuts with the cereal (high fat) will alter the digestion of the cereal (slow it down) and the glycemic index number will lower.

The following numbers were taken from *The New Glucose Revolution* by Jennie Brand-Miller, Ph.D., Thomas Wolever, MD, Ph.D., Kaye Foster-Powell, and Stephen Colagiuri, MD.

GL foods to limit (high numbers over 20)

Bagel	25
Corn Flakes	24
White Pasta	23
Raisins	28
Potato	26
White Rice	26
Risotto	36
Snickers Bar	23
Pancakes	39

GL foods (medium high numbers between 11-19)

Angel Food Cake	19
Banana	12
Dried Figs	16
English muffin	11
Sweet Potato	11
Brown Rice	16
Tortilla Chips	17
Yogurt	12

GL foods to have often (low numbers 10 or below)

Bran Cereal	4
Nuts	0
Apple	6
Oatmeal	9
Beans	8
Carrots	3
Grapes	8
Skim Milk	4

Gout

♦ Gout is a form of arthritis that is characterized by high levels of uric acid (one of the body's waste products) in the blood. Previous recommendations were to omit the amount of high purine-containing foods (purine is a precursor to uric acid) like organ meats, anchovies, and sardines. However, avoiding these foods has little impact on uric acid levels; current recommendations are therefore to maintain ideal weight, avoid consuming excessive alcohol, and drink at least two liters of fluids a day (preferably water, herbal tea, club soda, or low sodium vegetable juice). If this condition does not improve your doctor may prescribe medication.

Heart Disease

Heart disease is the number one killer in America. To reduce your risk of heart disease, it's important to follow these diet recommendations:

♦ Avoid over-consumption of saturated-fat foods (cheese, meat, high-fat dairy products, sauces, gravies, butter) and foods containing trans fat (mostly in processed foods with partially hydrogenated oils). These fats clog your arteries and encourage your liver to produce extra, more harmful cholesterol. Consume mostly monounsaturated-fat foods (olive oil, nuts, avocado). These fats increase healthy cholesterol and decrease unhealthy cholesterol levels.

♦ Eat high-fiber foods (at least four or five grams per serving) to total 30-50 grams each day. Build your fiber intake up gradually. Look for fiber in cereal, grains (kasha, barley, millet), fruits, vegetables, and beans.

◆ Consume cold-water fish that is high in omega-3 fats. This includes salmon, tuna, sardines, and mackerel. These omega-3 fats are found to thin blood, (therefore reducing clot formation and possibly a heart attack or stroke), boost good cholesterol and lower triglycerides. Fish is also an excellent replacement for higher-saturated-fat foods such as meat or poultry. You may also take up to 3,000 mg of fish oil daily.

◆ Take B vitamins, especially folic acid (B9) – 800 mcg, pyridoxine (B6) – 50-200 mg and Cobalamin (B12) – 6-60 mcg or up to 500 mcg. A multivitamin or a B-complex that contains the above amounts is necessary to reduce homocysteine levels (an amino acid found to increase the risk of heart disease when found in high levels in the blood).

◆ Flavonoids are antioxidants found in red grapes, blueberries, red wine, onions, citrus fruits, tomatoes, and black and green tea. Flavonoids thin blood and prevent damage from cholesterol.

◆ Antioxidants like vitamin C, E, selenium and betacarotene reduce free radical damage. Free radical damage may promote heart disease by stimulating blood to clot and plaque to build in the arteries. Free radicals are produced when oxygen is broken down by radiation exposure, air pollution, ozone, cigarette or cigar smoke, rancid fats or by-products of our foods and medications. They then allow disease to begin in our bodies. Oxidation in our bodies is similar to a rusted iron pipe. When a pipe is exposed to oxygen over time, it will rust. This rust is similar to the plaque buildup in our arteries. Antioxidants (anti-oxygen or against oxygen) do not allow oxygen to be broken down, so they neutralize these free radicals so they don't lead to diseases such as heart disease, cancer, arthritis, and aging by damaging the cells. Eating foods rich in whole grains, fruits, and vegetables is preferable in addition to taking vitamin C, E, beta-carotene and selenium supplements.

♦ Vitamin C (250-500 mg per day) or consume peppers, citrus fruits, broccoli, Brussels sprouts, cauliflower.

♦ Vitamin E (400 IU per day as d-alpha-tocopherol or d-mixed-tocopherols) or consume vegetable oils, almonds, soybeans, wheat germ, sunflower seeds.

♦ Beta-carotene (5,000-10,000 mg per day) or consume orange fruits and vegetables, dark leafy green vegetables, sweet potatoes, carrots, dried apricots, collard greens, spinach, kale.

♦ Selenium (100–200 mcg per day) or consume Brazil nuts, grains, seafood.

♦ Selenium and vitamin E taken together with a meal with some fat increases absorption in the body. Take apart from vitamin C, which may hinder absorption.

♦ Coffee: If it's brewed in French press machines, unfiltered or served as espresso, coffee maintains two compounds that may raise cholesterol. Cafestol and kahweol tend to raise LDL (lousy) cholesterol levels. Filtered coffee has not been shown to have these effects.

♦ Garlic has antioxidant properties. Onions, shallots and leeks, like garlic, are from the allium family and contain compounds to help prevent heart disease.

♦ Avoid over-consumption of animal protein. We only need approximately six to eight ounces of protein a day. Americans easily consume 15-20 ounces or more daily.

Most of the protein we consume comes from meat or poultry that contain the highest amounts of saturated fat and cholesterol. Substitute fish or soy products when possible, or combine beans and grains for a complete protein.

♦ Beware of fat-free foods. They usually contain more carbohydrates (sugar) and/or sodium. Excess sugar or carbohydrates turn into fat (triglycerides) since they can't be stored in abundance in the body. Choose low-fat food instead.

♦ Shellfish is a good choice. It has slightly higher amounts of sodium, but it has virtually *no saturated fat*! Shrimp and crayfish have higher levels of cholesterol than other shellfish. When compared to meat or poultry that do contain saturated fat, however, even the shrimp and crayfish come out on top. When you weigh out the portions typically eaten of shrimp vs. meat the cholesterol is identical. There is still the saturated fat issue, however. Saturated fat encourages the liver to produce more harmful cholesterol. Scallops have minimal cholesterol and are an even better choice.

♦ Sodium needs to be consumed in lower amounts. It may contribute to high blood pressure.

♦ Excess body weight certainly may contribute to heart disease, especially if stored in the chest and abdomen (apple shape).

♦ Metabolic syndrome or pre-diabetes puts a person at an increased risk of heart disease.

♦ Diabetes increases the risk of heart disease. If blood sugar is under control, the risk will decrease.

♦ Ask your doctor for the following blood tests to predict your heart disease risk: C-reactive protein, homocysteine, triglycerides, cholesterol (HDL/LDL), glucose, HbA1c and blood pressure.

Hypertension

Sodium is an electrolyte that is critical to maintaining fluid balance, normal muscle contraction and relaxation, and nerve transmission – all functions of the heart. High blood pressure is aggravated by increased salt consumption.

Blood pressure is the force exerted by the blood against the artery walls. The top number in a normal 120/60 reading is systolic pressure. This is the pressure when the heart contracts and pushes blood throughout the arteries. The bottom number is the diastolic pressure, which is the pressure in the arteries when the heart muscle relaxes between beats. Uncontrolled hypertension may lead to heart disease, stroke, and kidney disease.

What can you do to prevent hypertension?

- Lose weight if you're overweight (losing a mere 10 pounds can result in lower blood pressure!).
- Limit alcohol intake to moderate consumption: one drink per day (women) and two drinks per day (men). A drink is 12 oz. beer, 1-2 oz. liquor, or 4–6 oz. wine.
- Exercise at least 4-5 times a week for 30-60 minutes.
- Reduce sodium intake to no more than 2,400 mg per day. This is equivalent to approximately one teaspoon of salt. Remember, most foods contain sodium.
- Salt is sodium chloride. 40% from sodium, 60% from chloride.

- Maintain adequate amounts of potassium (try foods like apricots, bananas, beans, broccoli, cantaloupe, dates, figs, oranges, prunes, raisins, and tomatoes), magnesium (see *bone health* for list of foods) and calcium (see *bone health* for list of foods) intake to lower blood pressure.
- Reduce dietary saturated fat and cholesterol intake.
- Eat at least 30 grams of fiber each day.
- Avoid, or use sparingly, high-sodium foods like cold cuts, cheese, processed or convenience foods, canned foods (especially soups), olives, pickles, bouillon, soy sauce. Even light soy sauce contains 600 mg of sodium per tablespoon.
- A low-sodium food contains 140 mg per serving.
- Try *Mrs. Dash* or other spices instead of salt.
- Foods with blood pressure-lowering activity:
  - Celery or parsley (natural diuretic)
  - Fenugreek (high-fiber)
  - Fish oil (salmon, sardines, tuna)
  - Garlic, onions
  - Olive oil
  - Vitamin C foods (see vitamins)
  - Seafood

Hypoglycemia

What is it?
Reactive hypoglycemia usually occurs when your pancreas is overproducing insulin. Insulin is a hormone your pancreas makes to carry sugar (glucose) from your bloodstream to your body's cells to supply you with energy. In other words, it helps your body convert sugar into energy. If you produce too much insulin, you will carry too much sugar out of

the blood and the result will be hypoglycemia, otherwise known as low blood sugar. Hypoglycemia is defined as blood glucose levels below 50 mg/dL in those people with reactive hypoglycemia.

What are the symptoms?

You can tell how low your blood sugar is by testing it with a glucose monitor. There are obvious signs of low blood sugar, however. Sweating, hunger, shakiness, weakness, mental confusion, rapid heart rate, dizziness and blurred vision are some possible signs. If you have had hypoglycemia before, you may already know what your particular symptoms are.

How can I treat it?

Modifications of dietary carbohydrate help prevent hypoglycemia. Since carbohydrates turn 100% into sugar, they will stimulate insulin production. By overeating carbohydrates at one meal or snack (starches, fruits, milk), you will overproduce insulin and that will lead to hypoglycemia. An example of over-consumption might be a large bagel. The bagel is equal to 4 pieces of bread (60 grams of carbohydrates) or 5 tablespoons of sugar. Each 15 grams of total carbohydrate turn into 4 tsp. of sugar (1 Tbsp. + 1 tsp.) in the bloodstream. This is excessive if you tend to be hypoglycemic.

Dietary Guidelines

♦ Eat six small meals a day.
♦ Each time you eat, you should combine a high-fiber carbohydrate (oatmeal) with a good fat (walnuts) and/ or lean protein (cottage cheese). By combining foods

that help you digest slowly, you are slowing down the release of sugar into the bloodstream and therefore you are less likely to overproduce insulin.

♦ Do not eat more than 30 grams of total carbohydrate at one time.

♦ Avoid excessive intake of sugar in the form of sweets. These foods may stimulate excessive insulin release in persons with hypoglycemia because of their quick release of sugar into the bloodstream.

Irritable Bowel Syndrome

Approximately 40 million Americans – mostly women - have IBS (irritable bowel syndrome). IBS is a chronic disorder with symptoms that include abdominal bloating, pain and/or discomfort, and diarrhea or constipation. Most people with IBS have certain food sensitivities, therefore the following is recommended.

Treatment:

♦ Stay away from sugar alcohol. This includes any ingredient ending in "ol:" sorbitol, mannitol, xylitol, and so on. Sugar-free foods usually contain these ingredients.

♦ Stay away from artificial sweeteners such as aspartame (*Equal/NutraSweet*), saccharin (*Sweet 'N Low*), acesulfame potassium (*Ace K*), and sucralose (*Splenda*), usually contained in sugar-free foods.

♦ Stay away from fried foods and other fatty foods.

♦ Stay away from foods containing high fructose corn syrup.

♦ Stay away from chocolate, coffee, tea (unless herbal) and milk products. (Try almond, soy or rice milk or *Lactaid* milk – lactose free.)

♦ Don't overwhelm your digestive system! Consume smaller meals. Americans typically eat meals big enough for two or three people and wonder why they have digestive problems!

Try the following:
♦ Gradually increase fiber, especially fiber such as bran (insoluble fiber).
♦ Eat more wholesome foods and avoid processed, prepared foods.
♦ Drink water to flush the system and replace lost water from diarrhea.
♦ Take Acidophilus (a "good" bacteria to neutralize any "bad" bacteria in the intestines). Don't count on yogurt to have enough live cultures, since most of it is lost in the processing.
♦ Take chewable digestive or papaya enzymes to aid in digestion. Purchase acidophilus and digestive enzymes at a health food store or pharmacy.
♦ Try chamomile tea for relaxation of the digestive system.
♦ Exercise. Walk to stimulate the digestive system so it works efficiently.
♦ Breathe deeply to reduce stress caused by IBS.
♦ Try 1,000 – 3,000 mg of omega-3 fats in the form of fish oil, which acts as an anti-inflammatory. If you are on blood thinners such as Coumadin or aspirin, only consume omega-3 fats by eating cold-water fish.

Finally, pay attention to the times when you feel unwell, and think about what you ate, if you were stressed, and what else might have been going on. There may be certain trigger foods or situations that upset *your* system in particular.

Kidney Disease

Your kidneys are responsible for filtering waste and extra water from your blood in the form of urine. These bean-shaped organs also regulate blood pressure and calcium levels, and control production of red blood cells. Early kidney disease may have no symptoms.

Symptoms of more progressive kidney disease include:
♦ Swelling of hands or feet
♦ Puffy eyes
♦ Loss of appetite
♦ Fatigue
♦ Difficulty thinking clearly

Who's at risk?
♦ People with diabetes
♦ People with high blood pressure
♦ People with a family history of kidney disease

Treatment:
♦ Keep diabetes under strict control. Excessive sugar in the blood will make the kidneys work harder to filter it out. ACE inhibitors are commonly used to help prevent problems with the kidneys.
♦ Keep hypertension under control.
♦ Limit protein to no more than six ounces a day. Protein makes the kidneys work harder. Dairy, vegetable (soy) or fish are preferred sources of protein.

♦ Do not overeat high-sodium foods such as processed foods or convenience foods, cold cuts and soups.

♦ Reduce high-phosphorous foods like beans and wheat products.

♦ Reduce high-potassium foods like tomatoes and potatoes. You may leach a percentage of potassium out of potatoes by cutting them into quarters and soaking them in water for 3 hours or overnight.

♦ See a dietitian to advise a diet unique to your condition. You must focus on preserving the kidneys. At some point you may be required to have dialysis (a machine works to do the kidneys' job) or a kidney transplant.

Kidney Stones

Kidney stones are usually composed of calcium salts, uric acid or struvite. Calcium salts make up the majority of stones with uric acid or struvite being less likely. Years ago those with kidney stones were told to stay away from calcium. The recommendations have changed.

Kidney stones come from a diet made up of low fiber combined with a high intake of refined flours (white/processed flours), alcohol, animal protein, and fat. The most important thing you need to do is drink water. Stones will not form if the urine is diluted. Drink between eight and twelve eight-ounce glasses of water each day. Avoid high oxalate foods. Oxalate, not calcium, encourages stone formation. An abundance of oxalates are found in spinach, leeks, walnuts, chocolate, tea, beets, rhubarb, Swiss chard, and peanuts. Water is critical to drink in order to dilute urine.

If these are calcium-oxalate stones you need to cut back on sugar and increase potassium rich foods such as apricots, cantaloupe, bananas, avocados, peas, potatoes, trout, halibut, and tomatoes. You may eat calcium-rich foods such as milk, low-sodium cheese and yogurt. Luckily, calcium foods combine with oxalates and carry them out of the body. Do not take calcium supplements. Do not take vitamin C supplements, either, since studies are looking at the connection between large doses of vitamin C and kidney stones due to oxalate being a by-product of vitamin C metabolism.

Lactose Intolerance

Lactose is the sugar found in milk. If your body does not make any or enough lactase (the enzyme that processes lactose), the result is an inefficient breakdown of lactose or milk sugar. This creates stomach problems such as bloating, diarrhea, cramping, nausea, and/or flatulence. The simplest strategy is to take lactase drops or pills in order to supply your body with the enzyme you are lacking. You can also eliminate foods with lactose in them.

High-lactose foods:
Milk (all forms: regular, powdered, evaporated, sweetened, heavy cream, half-and-half)
Sour cream
White sauce
Cheese
Ice cream
Some yogurt

Also look for ingredients containing lactose that are found in some cold cuts, hot dogs, sausages, peanut butter, and convenience foods with milk products. In addition, some sugar substitutes contain lactose, for example: *Sweet n' Low, Equal*, dietetic candy, chewing gum, spices made with monosodium glutamate extenders.

Lactase enzyme is available in pill form or drops and is known as *Lactaid, Lactrase*, or *Dairy Ease*. It may be added to milk 24 hours before ingestion. In addition, a tablet form is available that can be ingested just before eating a meal containing lactose.

Check labels for lactose by looking for the terms milk, whey, and dry milk solids.

Supplemental drinks like *Boost* or *Ensure* are lactose-free.

Special commercially-prepared low-lactose foods, including milk, ice cream, and cottage cheese, are available in some supermarkets.

Lactobacillus acidophilus milk is better tolerated than milk, although there is individual variation.

Nuts

Go nuts with nuts, reasonably! They are high in both calories and nutrients so please use them and do not abuse them. Nuts offer many healthful benefits primarily from unsaturated fats, fiber, protein and carbohydrates plus they taste great.

Added to meals or snacks these nuts help to sustain the appetite and satisfy the desire to crunch while replacing the more typically consumed refined carbohydrate snack foods like pretzels and other chips that offer no nutritional value and simply encourage your appetite. Nuts have medicinal properties and have been shown to lower the risk of heart disease and help people with diabetes avoid fluctuating blood sugars. They may contribute to cancer prevention as well. A few nuts to mention are Brazil nuts that contain high amounts of selenium (an anti-cancer mineral), almonds that are high in fiber, calcium, and vitamin E and walnuts that are rich in omega-3 fats and ellagic acid for cancer prevention. Try to consume mostly raw, natural, or unsalted nuts.

Omega-3 Polyunsaturated Fats

Fish oils have been found to lower triglycerides, LDL (lousy) cholesterol, blood pressure and prevent blood clots. Omega-3s are important to consume in your diet since they are an essential fat that your body cannot produce. Consume at least one gram each day (1,000 mg) and up to 3 grams (3,000 mg). If you are currently taking Coumadin, aspirin or other blood-thinners like garlic, vitamin E, or Ginkgo Biloba do not take this in supplemental form unless approved by your doctor. Too many blood thinners can be dangerous!

The three types of omega-3 fats are:
1.   LNA (alpha-linolenic acid) is found in plant foods, especially walnuts, pumpkin and flaxseeds, soybeans, and oils such as canola, soybean, walnuts, pumpkin, and flax.

2.   EPA (eicosapentaenoic acid) is found in fish oil of cold-water fish.

3.   DHA (docosahexanoic acid) is found in fish oil.

You will receive omega-3 fats indirectly from LNA. The body needs to convert LNA into the more useable form of omega-3 fats known as EPA or DHA. This conversion is only 15% successful. Therefore, if you have to choose between a flax oil supplement and a fish oil supplement, fish oil is best. Be sure to purchase purified or distilled fish oil to avoid any contaminants. However, for extra fiber use flaxseed in its ground form – flaxseed meal – for greatest absorption. Use it in cereal and on top of yogurt as you would wheat germ.

Omega-3 fats in 3-ounce servings:

Herring	1.8 grams
Anchovies	1.8 grams
Salmon, canned	1.5 grams
Bluefin Tuna	1.3 grams
Sardines, canned	1.3 grams
Mackerel	1.1 grams
Sockeye salmon	1.1 grams
Swordfish	.90 grams
Oysters	.80 grams
Rainbow Trout	.75 grams
Tuna, canned	.65 grams
Sea bass	.65 grams

Triglycerides

Triglycerides help measure the risk of heart disease. They should be under 150 mg after a 12-hour fast. Very high triglycerides are typically associated with increased risk of heart disease as well as diabetes or pre-diabetes (a.k.a. insulin resistance, metabolic syndrome or syndrome X). Triglycerides are stored fats. They make up 90% of the fat in food and the fat stored in the body. Foods breakdown into sugar or glucose in varying degrees in the bloodstream. This sugar has to be used; otherwise, it is stored in the liver and muscle. Since storage space for sugar is limited in the body, the excess sugar turns into fat and gets stored as triglycerides.

To give fat-free foods a better taste, food manufacturers add extra sugar (total carbohydrate). Be sure to compare fat-free foods with low-fat foods. Usually, the carbohydrate and/or sugar on the food label will be a lot higher if fat is omitted. The result is the sugar in these fat-free foods turn into fat or triglycerides.

You can reduce triglyceride levels with a low-fat, high-fiber meal plan and few refined carbohydrates. Many studies show that by adding flaxseed meal to your diet it will help you to reduce triglycerides (see omega-3 fats). 3 grams (3,000 mg) of fish oil a day will work to lower triglycerides as a prescription drug might. Do not take more than 40% of your total calories from carbohydrates. Limit your alcohol consumption to three or four drinks per week and lose weight if you need to. Watch portion sizes. Remember that 1/3 cup cooked pasta or rice is already one serving of starch.

How many starch servings do you think you are having? (Most people are amazed to find how many servings they routinely consume!) Try not to exceed more than two or three starch servings at a meal. Otherwise, that starch will turn into too much sugar! And if you don't use this sugar for fuel it will ultimately turn into triglycerides or fat storage.

Vitamins

Vitamin A:

Get around 5,000 -10,000 IU per day of beta-carotene. This is a non-toxic form of vitamin A. Vitamin A is a fat-soluble vitamin that you get from foods such as carrots, sweet potatoes, apricots, cantaloupe and other orange fruits and vegetables as well as dark green leafy vegetables.

Vitamin B:

Get at least 400 to 800 mcg of folic acid (B9) for heart protection. You can take as much as 2 mg a day. Vitamin B is a water-soluble vitamin, so it's not as likely to become toxic in excessive doses. Take approximately 25 mg of Thiamin (B1) and/or eat fish, pork, soy, beans, peas, peanuts, and egg yolks. Take about 25 mg of Riboflavin (B2) and/or eat cold cereal, liver, salmon, milk, yogurt, eggs, and cheese. Take approximately 25 mg of Niacin (B3) and/or eat cold cereals, whole grains, breads, peanuts, chicken, fish, avocados, dates, figs, and prunes. Do not exceed 500 mg of niacin (if you are using it for heart disease prevention), since too much of it can cause liver damage. Take approximately 50 mg of Pyridoxine

(B6) and/or eat bananas, potatoes, spinach, soy, salmon, or tuna. Do not exceed 200 mg of B6, since too much can cause neurological problems. Take 6 mcg of Cobalamin (B12); if you are over 60 years of age, take 25 mcg to ensure adequate absorption and/or eat beef, pork, lamb, catfish, lobster, mussels, oysters, swordfish, tuna, eggs, milk, yogurt, or cheese. You may take up to 500 mcg of B12. A deficiency in this vitamin can cause nerve damage.

Vitamin C::

Take 250-500 mg twice a day. If you have a cold, try to take 1,000-3,000 mg per day and/or eat peppers, kiwis, citrus fruits, cantaloupe, strawberries, broccoli, sweet potato, parsley, and snow peas.

Calcium:

Persons 19-50 years of age should take 1,000 mg a day. Persons between 50 and 70 years of age should take 1,200 mg a day, and persons over 70 should take 1,500 mg. Take Calcium Citrate for best absorption with or without food. You must take Calcium Carbonate with meals to be absorbed. The body is only capable of absorbing 500 mg of calcium at one time so do not exceed that amount. The sun can provide adequate vitamin D if you are less than 60 years of age. If you are over 60, or live in areas with low sun exposure, take calcium with vitamin D (about 400 IU). If calcium makes you constipated then take it along with magnesium (about half the dose of the calcium you are taking). Magnesium will also help with calcium's absorption. Eight ounces of milk or yogurt, or one ounce of cheese will give you 300 mg of calcium. Don't take calcium at the same time as iron, since it inhibits the absorption of iron. If you eat many high-calcium foods such as milk, cheese, yogurt, or fortified foods with calcium such as orange juice, soy milk, tofu, fish and shellfish, rhubarb, spinach, almonds, figs, Brazil nuts, cashews, turnip greens, or kale, then cut back on the supplements.

Chromium:

Take 200 mcg per day. If you are trying to level out your blood sugar because you have diabetes, or are trying to control your appetite, then take up to 600 or 800 mcg per day. Over 1,000 mcg a day can be toxic. Eat clams, cheese, whole-grains, and/or brewers yeast.

Vitamin D:

Take 400 IU a day if you are under 70, and 600 IU if you are over 70. Eat foods like salmon or other fatty fish, fortified cereals, milk, eggs or get plenty of sunshine. If you are over 60 you will no longer absorb enough vitamin D from the sun.

Vitamin E:

Take 400 IUs of the natural form of vitamin E (also called d-alpha or d-mixed tocopherol). The synthetic – and less absorbable – version is dl-alpha or dl-mixed tocopherol. Vitamin E foods like wheat germ, apricots, almonds, hazelnuts, sunflower seeds, peanut butter, peaches and shrimp may also be eaten to increase vitamin E in the body.

Iron:

Take 0-10 mg if you are a man or postmenopausal woman. Children and premenopausal women may take up to 18 mg. If you become constipated reduce dose or increase magnesium to up to 600 mg. Don't take calcium at the same time as iron! Calcium inhibits the absorption of iron. If you eat a lot of red meat, try to take a multivitamin without iron, since excessive iron can be toxic to the liver. Besides liver and red meat (that contain the most absorbable forms the body can use), you may eat kelp, raisins, figs, carrots, beets, soybeans, bananas, asparagus, and sunflower seeds. Vitamin C foods help your body absorb iron more efficiently. You must consume these vitamin C foods within ½ hour of eating the food that contains iron. Example: cook a steak (iron) with peppers (vitamin C) or eat beans (iron) with mandarin orange slices (vitamin C) in a salad.

Magnesium:

Take at least 100 mg and up to 600 mg per day. Low magnesium levels may increase your risk of diabetes and heart disease. Eat whole grains, almonds, tuna, honey, pineapple, pecans, green vegetables and beans for magnesium.

Phosphorous:

Try to consume less than 1,000 mg daily. Too much phosphorous inhibits calcium absorption. We get too much from eating an abundance of protein in our diets. Excessive amounts of protein hinder the absorption of calcium and increase your risk of osteoporosis.

You may eat vegetable sources such as mushrooms, cashews, oats, beans, squash, pecans, carrots, and almonds.

Selenium:

Take 200 mcg. It can be toxic if you take over 1,000 mcg. Brazil nuts are very high in this cancer-protective mineral.

Zinc and Copper:

Take 15 – 20 mg of zinc and 2 mg of copper. Too much zinc will hinder copper absorption and possibly lead to anemia. Do not exceed 50 mg of zinc. Mushrooms, liver, seafood, soybeans, sunflower seeds, and brewer's yeast contain zinc. Soybeans, Brazil nuts, raisins, legumes, seafood, and blackstrap molasses all contain copper.

Coenzyme Q10 (CoQ10):

This powerful antioxidant enhances energy production of the heart. It has also been shown to be protective in heart disease, gum disease and cancer. The body manufactures this compound itself; however, many cholesterol-lowering drugs reduce the amount the body can make. Therefore, if you have heart disease or are taking cholesterol-lowering medications you should take 100 mg of CoQ10 in a liquid or gel form for best absorption. If you are taking it to prevent possible future problems, take 60 mg. If you are taking Coumadin (a blood thinner) don't take this antioxidant unless you check with your doctor first since it may reduce the effect of Coumadin. Spinach, broccoli and some fish contain small amounts of CoQ10.

Chapter Six: Everybody's Eating to Win

The Diet Game

by Randy Gossman

Meals Around the World

What is it about the traditional Mediterranean diet that is so healthy?

The *Mediterranean diet* is one of the healthiest diets you can follow. It consists primarily of whole grains, fruits, vegetables, fish, monounsaturated fats, beans, and other legumes and nuts.

♦ Rates of heart disease in the Mediterranean are 90% lower than in the United States. This seems to indicate that fat is not the culprit in heart disease, but perhaps the type of fat used is more important.
♦ The liberal use of olive oil, olives and other monounsaturated fats can raise HDL (healthy cholesterol) and lower LDL (lousy cholesterol).
♦ Olive oil or olives contain squalene, which is a phytochemical that inhibits tumor formation in the lungs, pancreas and breast.
♦ This liberal oil use can also sustain the appetite and energy level.
♦ Extra-virgin olive oil contains phenolic compounds that act as antioxidants. They are both cancer and heart protective.
♦ Saturated fats like butter are replaced with monounsaturated fats like olive oil.
♦ The traditional Mediterranean diet has virtually no partially hydrogenated or trans fats, which are as unhealthy as saturated fats. This is due to the use of fresh foods and the lack of fast foods, convenience or processed foods.

♦ Meats are replaced with fish that contain healthy omega-3 fats.
♦ Nuts contain omega-3 fats and other heart-protective properties.
♦ 30-42% of the diet is from fat, mostly heart-healthy fats.
♦ Many herbs used traditionally are cancer fighters. Rosemary and parsley are two such herbs.
♦ Fresh fruits and vegetables are consumed often. They are natural cancer fighters. Apricots, broccoli, Brussels sprouts, cauliflower, garlic, onions, oranges, and tomatoes are frequently eaten.
♦ Beans and other legumes contain high fiber. These are used in soups, salads or in casseroles.
♦ There is moderate wine drinking in the Mediterranean. Studies show that moderate drinking will significantly lower one's risk for heart disease.
♦ Living a less stressful life also will decrease your risk for heart disease!

What is it about the traditional Chinese diet that is so healthy?

The *Chinese diet* in its traditional sense results in lower cancer rates. However, hypertension rates are high. Unfortunately, the Chinese diet is growing more similar to the American diet and disease rates are following.

♦ The Chinese consume fresh fruits, vegetables and grains and smaller amounts of meat, poultry, and fish.
♦ Tea (green or black) is a traditional beverage of choice in China. It contains cancer-protective antioxidants. Drinking three to five cups a day is heart-protective and staves off cancer.

♦ Sodium is the problem in the Chinese diet. MSG (monosodium glutamate) and soy sauce are used in abundance here. As little as one tablespoon of soy sauce contains 900 mg of sodium. Even light soy sauce contains 600 mg per tablespoon. People are advised to consume fewer than 3,000 mg of sodium per day.

♦ The cancer-fighting vegetables that are amply consumed are cruciferous vegetables such as cabbage, bok choy, mustard greens, and broccoli.

♦ Although in general a Chinese meal includes white rice and vegetables, you may want to use brown rice to incorporate more fiber and vitamins that are lost during the processing of white rice.

♦ Dairy products are rarely consumed here. Osteoporosis rates are low in China, possibly due to the fact that soy products such as bean curd provide high levels of calcium. In addition, excessive protein leaches calcium out of the body. In China, protein is consumed in amounts as small as three ounces each day!

♦ Fat is used sparingly in stir-fry dishes.

♦ Do soy's phytoestrogens protect women from developing breast or ovarian cancer? The lower cancer rates in China may be the result of replacing meats and poultry with bean curd, or perhaps it's the antioxidant effects of the tea.

What is it about the traditional French diet that is so healthy?

The *French diet* appears to be unhealthy, with an abundance of saturated fat from cheese, refined carbohydrate baguettes with butter or pastries, and pate; however, these people are indeed healthy.

♦ The rate of cancer and heart disease are lower in France than in the United States, possibly due to the high consumption of fresh fruits and vegetables, and smaller portions used by the French.

♦ They consume approximately 35% of fat daily – typically saturated fat.

♦ They do not snack often. When they do snack, it is on fruit and only occasionally do they indulge in their famous pastries. Perhaps it is due to their high fat consumption and large midday meal that they feel full longer and they do not require snacks.

♦ Moderate alcohol consumption in France may decrease the incidence of heart disease. However, some do drink excessively. This may explain why rates of liver diseases such as cirrhosis of the liver appear to be higher.

♦ The French eat their largest meal at lunch. They also consume smaller portions when dining at home or at restaurants. This may help to explain the low (8%!) obesity rate in France.

♦ Abstaining from cheese and butter is usually the French way to watch calories. They don't use the commercial diet meals or drinks sold in abundance in the United States.

♦ The French most frequently use fresh ingredients. They don't abuse fast foods, convenience or prepared foods like Americans regularly do.

♦ They are not obsessed with their eating or their weight. This results in a low incidence of obesity.

What is it about the traditional Japanese diet that is so healthy?

The *Japanese diet* consists of many healthy foods and preparation techniques. When you think of the Japanese diet you immediately think of seaweed, tea, low-fat, high-sodium, fish, sushi, white rice, and soy. (I think of Sake!)

♦ The lowest rates of heart disease, breast cancer, type 2 diabetes and the highest life expectancy are seen in Japan.

♦ They have the highest rates of stomach cancer, probably due to the high amounts of sodium used. Pickled foods, soy sauce, smoked and salted foods are frequent. Heterocyclic amines and other toxic chemicals are found in their foods. This may also be responsible for the increased risk of stomach cancer.

♦ They consume relatively low-fat diets. 26% of their calories for the day come from fat.

♦ Some of that 26% of fat comes from heart-healthy omega-3 fats from the abundance of fish eaten in Japan. Nori, the seaweed surrounding sushi rolls, provides calcium and omega-3 fats as well.

♦ Soy products containing cancer protective isoflavones and phytoestrogens seem to significantly lower the incidence of breast and prostate cancer.

♦ Seaweed like hiziki and nori are consumed regularly. These seaweeds contain high levels of sodium but they are also extremely high in calcium. Sodium may increase hypertension, but calcium may decrease it.

♦ Green tea also adds heart and cancer protection to the Japanese diet.

♦ Sake is an alcoholic beverage of choice in Japan known as "rice wine." It is served hot or cold.

What is it about the current Scandinavian diet that is so healthy?

The *Scandinavian diet* was once responsible for a very high incidence of heart disease. The high saturated-fat consumption was partly responsible. In addition, the former method of brewing coffee by boiling it without a filter allowed the formation of cafestol and kahweol, two substances that increase cholesterol. However, as the diet is changing, so is the risk of heart disease. The risk of cancers such as breast, lung, prostate and colorectal is at a minimum in Scandinavian countries.

♦ High fiber is consumed by eating whole-grain breads, especially rye and pumpernickel breads, cereals, and other grains.
♦ Due to the abundance of low-fat dairy products that are now being consumed there is a lower incidence of hypertension, osteoporosis, colon cancer (fiber also aides in preventing this), breast cancer and kidney stones.
♦ Although in the past fruits and vegetables weren't abundantly available, they are now being imported frequently.
♦ The grain, rye, is a staple in Scandinavian countries.
♦ Berries are frequently served for dessert. Lingonberries are berries grown locally and contain high fiber and vitamin C.

What is it about the traditional West African diet that is so healthy?

♦ The *West African diet* is responsible for providing their people with the lowest cancer rates in the world.

♦ This diet is filled with mostly fruits, vegetables, grains, beans and small amounts of meat. They often consume dense, high-fiber vegetables like sweet potatoes. Sweet potatoes are one of the most nutrient-dense vegetables available. They provide vitamin A in the form of beta-carotene, vitamin C, potassium and fiber.

♦ Hot and spicy foods dominate this diet due to the abundance of hot peppers grown there.

♦ Vegetable stews are often prepared. These stews include a host of disease-fighting foods and are hot and spicy. They include small amounts of meat for flavoring. Some vegetables often used are onions, tomatoes, carrots, potatoes, cabbage, eggplant, plantains, yams, lima beans, butter beans, okra, gourd, pumpkin and squash.

♦ Peanuts are eaten in abundance. They contain beta-sitosterol, a substance found to inhibit tumor growth, which may be somewhat responsible for the low rates of cancer. They also contain resveratrol – a heart healthy antioxidant.

♦ The fat used here comes from tropical oils such as palm oil. This is a saturated fat that can contribute to higher cholesterol levels. This can be counteracted with all the fresh fruits, vegetables and other fiber packed foods. (The above information was used in combination with "30 Secrets of the World's Healthiest Cuisines" by Steven Jonas, MD and Sandra Gordon.)

Chapter Seven: My Favorite Things

The Diet Game

by Randy Gossman

My Favorite Foods

- *Nature's Own* 100% Whole-wheat Bread (low-calorie/high-fiber)
- *Barbara's Bakery Crackers* (no Trans fat or partially/hydrogenated fats)
- *Kame Crackers* (no Trans fat or partially/hydrogenated fats)
- *Hains Oyster Crackers* (no Trans fat or partially/hydrogenated fats)
- Baked tortilla chips, baked potato chips, pretzels
- Single serving microwaveable popcorn
- *Health Valley* Soup: Split Pea, Black Bean, Lentil, 5-Bean
- *Tabatchnick* products: soup and vegetarian chili (high-fiber)
- *Imagine* Soup (no dairy)
- Whole-wheat matzo (high-fiber – look for brands with 4 grams/slice)
- Kashi's *Good Friends* Cereal (the original with 6 grams of sugar/8 grams of fiber and 90 calories for ¾ cup)
- Kashi's *Heart to Heart* (5 grams of fiber per ¾ cup)
- Kashi's *Go Lean* (10 grams of fiber per ¾ cup plus soy protein)
- Shredded Wheat n' Bran (8 grams of fiber per 1 ¼ cup)
- *Quaker* or Irish 100% rolled oats (oatmeal)
- Canned beans (look for lowest sodium brand and rinse well)
- *Healthy Harvest* whole-wheat pasta
- Walnuts and pumpkin seeds (high in heart-protective omega-3 fats)
- Almonds (high in fiber and calcium)
- Pecans (good antioxidants)
- Cashews (good antioxidants)

- Blueberries, real grape juice and red grapes (all are high in resveratrol, a heart-healthy antioxidant)
- Low-sodium V-8 juice or tomato juice (lycopene)
- *Cabot* Monterey Jack 50% or 75% reduced-fat cheese
- Jarlsberg light cheese (low-sodium, low-fat, and great taste)
- *Chavrie* goat cheese (lower fat, sodium, cholesterol)
- *Veggie Slices* soy cheese (look for lower sodium flavors)
- *Parmalat Skim Milk Plus* (creamy, higher in calcium and no BGH-bovine growth hormone-injected cows are used)
- *Silk* soy milk (plain or vanilla)
- Extra virgin, cold-pressed olive oil (low in saturated fat and high in monounsaturated fat)
- Cold-pressed canola oil (omega-3 fats, low in saturated fat and high in monounsaturated fat)
- 25-calorie Nestle's *Fat Free Hot Cocoa*
- *Alba 70* (70-calorie chocolate malted if made with water and ice)
- *Friendship* low-fat cottage cheese (also available in lower sodium)
- *Walden Farms No Calorie* salad dressing
- *Ken's* Light Chunky Blue Cheese or Light Northern Italian dressing
- *Paul Newman's* Light Italian Dressing
- Seasoned rice vinegar
- Balsamic vinegar
- Light Ginger Dressing
- *Just For 2* Wishbone salad dressing
- *Maple Groves Light Caesar* salad dressing
- *Maple Groves Vermont* sugar-free syrup
- *Morningstar Farms* Chik Nuggets (soy nuggets)

- *Morningstar Farms* Low-fat Garden Patties (lots of vegetables, low-fat)
- *Morningstar Farms* Buffalo Wings (soy nuggets – spicy!)
- *Gardenburger* Riblets and Meatballs (soy versions)
- *Smart Dogs* (lower sodium vegetarian/soy hot dog)
- Sugar-free chocolate fudgsicles (low carbohydrates)
- Sugar-free tropical fruit bars (low carbohydrates)
- Starbucks' 120-calorie mocha low-fat pops
- *Healthy Choice* Ice Cream (tasty and low-fat)
- *Land O' Lakes* light whipped butter
- *Smart Balance* light margarine
- Hummus dip or baba ghanouj
- *Stonyfield Farms* fat-free vanilla or fruit yogurt
- *Classico* tomato and basil sauce
- Crepes (plain and located in produce department)
- *Eggland's Eggs* (lower cholesterol in this higher quality egg)
- *Go Lean* frozen blueberry or multi-grain waffles (high fiber)
- Dried apricots/cooked tomatoes (lycopene)
- Peppers (high in vitamin C)
- Avocado (healthy monounsaturated fat)
- Broccoli sprouts (like alfalfa sprouts except much healthier: like eating bunches of broccoli)
- Unprocessed oat bran or wheat bran (to add to ice cream, yogurt or cereal for additional fiber)
- *Bigelow* Red Raspberry Iced Tea
- *Marjon* firm tofu
- Sweet potatoes
- Kasha
- Bulgur
- Barley
- Brown or wild rice

My Favorite Workouts

◆ Denise Austin: www.deniseaustin.com

  ◆ Get Fit Faster Arms and Shoulders
  ◆ Power Kickboxing
  ◆ Best of Hit the Spot

◆ Tamilee Webb: www.naturaljourneys.com

  ◆ I Want Those Buns
  ◆ 10 Minute Buns
  ◆ Tighter Assets Weight loss

◆ Billy Blanks: www.taebo.com

  ◆ Ultimate Lower Body Tae Bo
  ◆ Basic Tae Bo
  ◆ Tae Bo Cardio
  ◆ Tae Bo Flex

◆ Gin Miller: www.ginmiller.com

  ◆ Reebok Intense Moves (Step Interval Training)

For additional workout tapes: call 800-433-6769 or go to www.CollageVideo.com

My Favorite Newsletters and Websites

Eating Well Magazine
www.eatingwell.com

Harvard Health Letter
www.health.harvard.edu

Nutrition Action Newsletter
www.cspinet.org

Self-Healing (Dr. Andrew Weil)
www.drweilselfhealing.com

Ask Dr. Weil questions
www.drweil.com

Tufts University Health and Nutrition
www.healthletter.tufts.edu

Weill Medical College of Cornell University: Women's Health Advisor
1-800-847-7131

My Favorite Health Books

The ABC Clinical Guide to Herbs
Mark Blumenthal
Founder and Executive Director
American Botanical Council (ABC)

This Organic Life: Confessions of a Suburban Homesteader
Joan Dye Gussow, Ed.D
Mary Swartz Rose Professor Emeritus of Nutrition
Education and *my* former professor of Nutrition at
Teachers College, Columbia University

Encyclopedia of Natural Supplements
Michael Murray, N.D.

Encyclopedia of Natural Medicine
Michael Murray, N.D.
Leading researcher in the field of natural medicine and a
faculty member of Seattle's Bastyr University, and Joseph
Pizzorno, N.D., naturopathic physician, researcher, and
educator and founding president of Bastyr University

Food Politics: How the Food Industry Influences Nutrition and Health
Marion Nestle, Ph.D, MPH
Professor and Chair, Department of Nutrition and Food
Studies, New York University, New York

Fast Food Nation: The Dark Side of the All-American Meal
Eric Schlosser, Author

Eat, Drink, And Be Healthy
Walter C. Willet, M.D.
Chairman of the Department of Nutrition at the Harvard School of Public Health and Professor of Medicine at the Harvard Medical School

Eating Well For Optimum Health
Andrew Weil, M.D.
Director of The Program in Integrative Medicine and Clinical Professor of Medicine at the University of Arizona

Physician's Desk Reference (PDR) for Herbal Medicines
Based on German Federal Authority's Commission E (the governmental body widely recognized as having conducted the most authoritative evaluation of herbs in the world)

Chapter Eight: Winning your Points

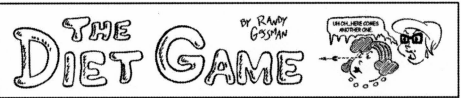

Food, Exercise and Feelings Journal

B= breakfast L= lunch D= dinner S= snack

Before you begin to keep records, ask yourself the following questions:

1.   What image do you see when you look in the mirror? Describe it.

2.   Are you happy with that person or would you like to change something?

3.   Do you feel you have the ability to change that something?

4.   Do you fear having any illnesses?

5.   What do you wish to do when you lose weight?

6.   What stops you from working hard in order to reach your weight loss goal?

7.   How does overeating make you feel?
     At the moment, the next day or week?

8.   Have you had goals in the past about career, relationships, etc., that you have reached?

9.   How did you accomplish them? Why did you fail or succeed?

10. What thoughts go through your mind as you are making poor choices?

Sample:
B= Breakfast, L= Lunch, D= Dinner, S= Snack

Sun	FOOD: # of Carbs, Protein, Fat
B	1 cup cooked oatmeal (2 C) ¾ cup berries (1 C) 2 walnuts (1 F)
L	Small Salad 2 Tbsp. light dressing (1 F) ½ cup chickpeas (1 C) (1 P) 2 ounces salmon (2 P)
D	3 cups broccoli and spinach (2 C) 5 ounces fish grilled (5 P)
S	11:00 am 1 small apple (1 C)
	3:00 pm 12 cashews (2 F)
	9:00 pm 1 fruit (1 C)

EXERCISE	Points for today: 20
TYPE	Kickboxing
TIME (S)	5:00 – 6:00 pm

FEELINGS	
Full/hungry	I get hungry if I don't eat every 3 hours
Satisfied/ tempted	Mixing fat and carbs satisfies my appetite
Positive/ negative	I feel more energetic when combining foods
Motivated/ depressed	I feel motivated to reach my goals
Other	Feeling healthy is worth all the work!

M	FOOD
B	
L	
D	
S	

EXERCISE	Points for today:
TYPE	
TIME (S)	

FEELINGS	
Full/hungry	
Satisfied/ tempted	
Positive/ negative	
Motivated/ depressed	
Other	

Tu	FOOD
B	
L	
D	
S	

EXERCISE	Points for today:
TYPE	
TIME (S)	

FEELINGS	
Full/hungry	
Satisfied/ tempted	
Positive/ negative	
Motivated/ depressed	
Other	

W	FOOD
B	
L	
D	
S	

EXERCISE	Points for today:
TYPE	
TIME (S)	

FEELINGS	
Full/hungry	
Satisfied/ tempted	
Positive/ negative	
Motivated/ depressed	
Other	

Th	FOOD
B	
L	
D	
S	

EXERCISE	Points for today:
TYPE	
TIME (S)	

FEELINGS	
Full/hungry	
Satisfied/ tempted	
Positive/ negative	
Motivated/ depressed	
Other	

Marci Page Sloane MS, RD, LD/N, CDE

F	FOOD
B	
L	
D	
S	

EXERCISE	Points for today:
TYPE	
TIME (S)	

FEELINGS	
Full/hungry	
Satisfied/tempted	
Positive/negative	
Motivated/depressed	
Other	

Sa	FOOD
B	
L	
D	
S	

EXERCISE	Points for today:
TYPE	
TIME (S)	

FEELINGS	
Full/hungry	
Satisfied/ tempted	
Positive/ negative	
Motivated/ depressed	
Other	

Su	FOOD
B	
L	
D	
S	

EXERCISE	Points for today:
TYPE	
TIME (S)	

FEELINGS	
Full/hungry	
Satisfied/ tempted	
Positive/ negative	
Motivated/ depressed	
Other	

The Diet Game

by Randy Gossman

Our ultimate goal in life is to be happy. Overindulgence in food does not make us happy; it only gives us a temporary feeling of pleasure. However, this immediate pleasure will lead to illness and obesity. We feel that we deserve to eat well because we live a hard life. We really deserve to be happy. We will feel happiest if we are healthy, can fit into our clothes comfortably and if we accomplish our goals. Please think before you eat. We must always involve thought in our choices. Do not eat without thinking of the consequences. Eat with a conscience. Review and understand the overall concept of eating introduced to you in *The Diet Game*.

Here's to your healthier and happier life!
Eat and be well…
Marci

Index

A

B

C

D

H

I

P

R

S

W

X

Z

About The Author

Marci Sloane, MS, RD, LD/N, CDE is a Registered Dietitian/Nutritionist and Certified Diabetes Educator who holds a double Masters of Science degree in Nutrition and Physiology from Columbia University. A popular lecturer, she has appeared on radio talk shows, teaches nutrition on-line to the Art Institute's students and manages JFK Medical Center's Diabetes and Nutrition Education Center where she counsels both groups and individuals. Her passion and humor help to teach and motivate you to stay healthy for life! In her spare time she indulges her musical talents of singing, playing guitar and piano and writing songs. Marci resides in Boca Raton, Florida with her husband, Jon, and four cats Pinky, Floyd, Wakoda, and Ozzy.

Printed in the United States
37380LVS00003B/58-75